CONTEMPORARY
SCULPTURE
TECHNIQUES

MORTAL COMBAT by John Baldwin

WELDED STEEL

*(Mr. and Mrs. York Wilson Collection,
Toronto, Canada)*

IN MEMORIAM (detail) by John Baldwin

FIBERGLASS

(Photograph by Doug Stewart)

CONTEMPORARY SCULPTURE TECHNIQUES

Welded Metal and Fiberglass

John Baldwin

Photographic supervision: Doug Stewart

Reinhold Publishing Corporation
A subsidiary of Chapman-Reinhold, Inc.
New York Amsterdam London

ACKNOWLEDGMENTS

I wish to express my gratitude to the many museums, galleries, collectors, artists and students who permitted me to reproduce their works. I also want to extend my gratitude to the Owens-Corning Fiberglas Corporation, Inter-chemical Corporation-Finishes Division, and North American Aviation Corporation for their assistance.

The Art Library staff at Ohio University was most co-operative, as were Professor of Chemistry, Jessie Day and Professor of Design, Charles L. Smith.

I am especially indebted to my friend James Norman Schmidt for his many readings of the manuscript and the many valuable suggestions he made. A book of this kind is impossible without the close co-operation of a fine photographer. One look at Doug Stewart's photographs will convince the reader of my indebtedness to him.

Finally, I wish to express my thanks to that one person who, throughout this effort was typist, illustrator, indispensable girl Friday and solace, Bunny, my wife, to whom I dedicate this book.

© 1967, Reinhold Publishing Corporation
All rights reserved
Printed in the United States of America
Library of Congress Catalog Card Number: 67-14152
Designed by Dorothy U. Lewis
Typeset by M. J. Baumwell
Printed by The Comet Press, Inc.
Published by Reinhold Publishing Corporation
430 Park Avenue, New York, N.Y.
A subsidiary of Chapman-Reinhold, Inc.

CONTENTS

PREFACE

Sculpture, a major art, is experiencing a renaissance in the twentieth century. New techniques and materials account for much of this new spirit and vitality. This book deals with two of the most important and revolutionary techniques affecting sculpture today — welded metals and fiberglass reinforced plastics.

The text, while brief, provides sufficient technical data and background information to complement the step by step photographic illustrations of these new methods. The diagrams are presented as simplified graphic substitutes for the very complex chemical and mechanical processes involved in reinforced plastics and metal welding. There are also many examples of finished sculpture in black and white and color showing the wide variety of work being produced with these modern techniques.

This book is intended as a guide for the student of sculpture who is eager to begin but dismayed by the complex nature of these new mediums. It is also intended to encourage those artists who have been aware of the great possibilities of these new techniques but reluctant to make the switch. The information presented should also interest devotees and collectors of sculpture who want to be informed about these two important techniques that are changing the character of sculpture today.

PART I

INTRODUCTION:

The Physical and Technical Nature of Sculpture

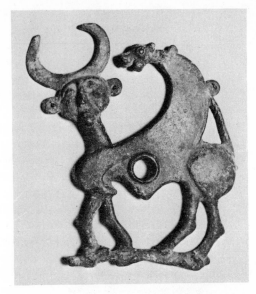

Luristan Horse-bit Plate about 1200 B.C.

BRONZE – One of a pair in the form of a human-headed winged bull.

(Courtesy of the Denver Art Museum)

The Heritage

New carbon dating techniques indicate that the world is far older than we had previously believed and that man was altering his environment long before the Garden of Eden had been thought to exist. Since the years given to the average mortal are so very few, fifty thousand or twenty five thousand or even five thousand years are equally incomprehensible spans of time. Therefore, it is enough to know that man has been making art objects for eons. Because some of the materials used were of impermanent substance — soluble, flammable, and subject to slow decay— most of the works have disappeared. The remaining sculpture and artifacts, or fragments of these, are in most instances our only record of man's earliest history.

The impulse to shape, model or form is fundamental to man's nature. He creates three-dimensional objects either by scratching and carving a hard substance with a still harder instrument, by modeling a plastic material with fingers and hands, or by joining mechanically a complex of related elements. Ancient civilized man carried this impulse to fantastic heights of achievement along the Nile, in the Tigris-Euphrates valley, in the Eastern Mediterranean, Central and South America, and throughout the Orient. Carved stone, hammered metals, glazed ceramic, glass, and cast bronze were the durable media of these largely unknown artisans whose legacy of craftsmanship has inspired many artists and has driven others to despair.

Ancient craftsmen, trained in the tradition of their culture, carefully passed on their skills from generation to generation, permitting little change or deviation. Technical secrets were handed down from father to son or kept within a specialized community whose only purpose was to carve the stone, beat the gold, or to form and fire the clay. Art was a group activity and we shall never know the names of the many thousands of individuals who left us something of their skill.

A few names have come down to us from the ancient world—Myron, Praxiteles and Phidias for example—but it was not until the Renaissance that numerous artists gained recognition for their individual achievements. Works by Donatello, Cellini and Michelangelo are frequently offered as evidence of the superiority of Renaissance craftmanship, but these are only a few of the many great masters who proudly signed their works and taught their skills to worthy apprentices.

DAVID by Michelangelo

MARBLE — Accademia, Florence

(Courtesy of Alinari Art Reference Bureau)

Polychromed Figure Proto-Toltec, about A.D. 500

TERRA COTTA

(Courtesy of Miguel J. Malo)

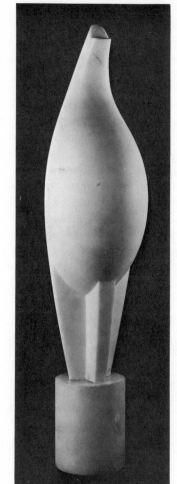

BIRD by Constantin Brancusi, 1912

MARBLE

(Courtesy of the Philadelphia Museum of Art. The Louise and Walter Arensberg Collection)

Technique

> What distinguishes the artist from the dreamer is his plastic sensibility, his capability in manipulating materials, above all, his sense of form.
>
> HERBERT READ

Technique is a part of the creative process. Through the mastery of techniques the sculptor is able to form intractable materials and imbue them with spirit and vitality. A sculptor cannot conceive of a work without taking into account the materials and techniques he will use. The medium selected, whether clay, wood, stone, plastics or steel, largely determines the general form, while the techniques provide its special form. One can do things with clay that are not practical in wood, while steel permits the creation of forms not feasible in clay. There is also an aesthetic principle involving "truth to materials." Henry Moore, in stating this idea, said that stone, being hard and concentrated "...should not be falsified to look like soft flesh." Herbert Read writing about Moore in *The Philosophy of Modern Art* said, "the aim of the sculptor like Henry Moore is to represent his conceptions in the forms natural to the material he is working in." Read stressed this "truth to materials" still further when he said, "What is important is that the effects of one set of tools on one kind of material should not be imitated in another material by another set of tools."

Another reason for the sculptor's preoccupation with materials and techniques is the predominantly physical nature of sculpture. While painting presents only an illusion of physical forms in space, sculpture is a real, three-dimensional structure — a free standing form with weight and mass—that must obey the laws of gravity. There are many technically inferior paintings that hang on the walls of museums and galleries, but the slow disintegration of the pigments and ground does not limit our perception of the painted image for a considerable length of time. Leonardo's "Last Supper" has been in a state of disintegration since 1494. A piece of sculpture, on the other hand, if not properly executed, will collapse in an instant. Even in its earliest stages, as raw material, it must be properly supported, balanced or contained. The contemporary sculptor George Sugarman stated in a recent panel discussion, ". . . my sculpture, like any other sculpture, has the engineering problem of supporting itself . . . sculpture is, in part, engineering."

Technique should never become an end in itself. It should always remain a means to an end. Technique is the means by which a sculptural idea is carried from a vague mental conception to a tangible, three-dimensional reality. An understanding of the characteristics of a given medium, such as the plasticity of clay or the grain of a particular wood, facilitates a dialogue between the artist and his material. Once involved, the artist is able to lose himself in his work—to be completely carried away, transported, so to speak —. thus freeing his creative impulses. Hans Arp has said, "Art is a fruit growing out of man like the fruit out of a plant, like the child out of the mother."

There are a few who believe that the simplest and quickest way to work a material is the best and that spontaneity alone guarantees success. In the struggle to control a medium—to form it to one's needs — changes in the original concept may occur. What seemed *great* at the outset, may later prove impractical, uninteresting or trite. Through the slow, painstaking processes of building up or cutting down, time may work in the artist's favor. He has time to reevaluate the image and time to simplify and clarify the forms. Constantin Brancusi said, "it is while carving stone that you discover the spirit of your material and the properties peculiar to it. Your hand thinks and follows the thoughts of the material."

RECLINING FIGURE by Henry Moore

ELM WOOD

(Courtesy of Albright-Knox Art Gallery, Buffalo, New York. Room of Contemporary Art Fund)

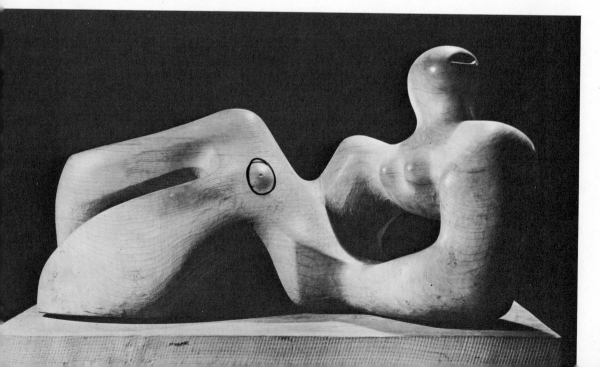

David Hostetler, sculptor,
carving wood. His
sculpture, *American Wife,*
elm wood, is in foreground.

(Photograph by Jon Webb)

Traditional Media and Techniques

The traditional techniques of sculpture have changed very little over the centuries. The hand tools of today's carvers are essentially the same as those used by the carvers of the Sphinx. Metal chisels were pounded then as now with mallets. Jewel-tipped drills and abrasives were used in much the same way as sculptors use them today. Wood was carved with a small adz and probably finished with metal blades and abrasives. Terra cotta figures dating back to prehistoric times give evidence of the antiquity of modeling and firing plastic earth. Bronzes of exquisite beauty and technical skill from ancient China and Egypt indicate that metal casting techniques had been developed to such a high level that they are still unsurpassed in spite of our mechanical advantages.

Traditionally, sculpture is divided into modeling and carving. That which is modeled is additive and that which is carved is subtractive. In principle,

carving is the easiest technique to comprehend though by no means the easiest to master. The carver attacks a block of hard material, usually stone or wood, with chisels and mallet; slowly and painstakingly he chips away all of the excess material until the desired form is revealed. This is the most direct method, since the work is complete once the form is realized by directly carving it from the original block. There is no further process necessary to make it more permanent or durable. The finished sculpture is as durable as the stone or wood from which it was carved.

The stones and woods for sculpture vary in hardness, texture, grain and color. The carver who is familiar with these characteristics will conceive of a suitable form, one that lends itself to the qualities inherent in the material. These qualities are considered not only in the planning stage but throughout

11

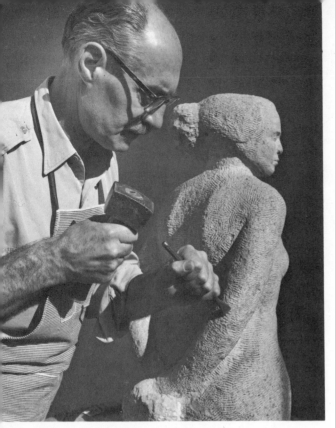

Frederick Taylor, sculptor, carving stone

(Photograph by the author)

the carving process. It is because of this direct involvement with a very demanding medium and the aesthetic attraction of the material that carving continues to hold such an appeal for so many sculptors today.

Modeling, on the other hand, is as unlike carving as any two methods can be. Where carving is a continual reduction of mass, modeling is a process of building it up. In place of the hard, rigid, resistant materials of the carver, the modeler uses soft, plastic media such as clay or plaster. These materials are relatively impermanent in their hard, dry state and therefore they are usually used only as a means of achieving a form that will be cast later in a more durable material. This is why modeling is considered to be an indirect method.

Sculpture modeled in a plastic medium does not have the same restrictions as sculpture carved in hard wood or stone, nor does it have the same formal potential. The plasticity of the modeling media makes complex and fluid forms easy to achieve but the instability of the material imposes a limitation that must be considered. The plastic consistency of modeling materials requires only simple, spatula-like

Bronze Foundry. Pouring molten bronze into the investment.

(Photograph by the author)

SENTINEL by Lothar Kestenbaum
CAST BRONZE BY THE LOST-WAX PROCESS

tools of various shapes and sizes. Furthermore, the artist may use his hands and fingers more than he uses his tools to form the material. Being soft and plastic, the clay, wet plaster or other modeling materials are usually built up on an armature of metal or wood. Without this support the forms would collapse of their own weight. The potter's techniques of throwing cylindrical clay forms on a wheel or building them up with slabs and coils are also used for sculpture.

If the finished modeled sculpture is to be carried through other processes to insure permanence, the limitations as well as the advantages of these techniques must also be considered by the artist. The simplest way to make modeled clay durable is to fire it in a kiln.

It is then called terra cotta (baked earth). This process fuses the particles of the clay by heating it to a temperature between 1000° and 3000°F. Another way of achieving permanence is to make a mold of the soft clay or wax form and cast it in a more durable material such as plaster or cement.

The most involved method of making modeled sculpture permanent is to cast it in metal. There are two methods of metal casting: sand casting and lost-wax casting. Basically, sand-mold casting consists of tamping damp sand around a pattern, removing the pattern and then filling the negative space in the sand with molten metal.

The lost-wax method, which has been traditionally the metal casting process for the production of fine works of art, is extremely complex. It involves many steps—from making a wax pattern of the original, fitting it with a system of wax sprues, runners and vents—to investing it with a refractory material of plaster, sand and asbestos. The wax is melted out of the investment, leaving spaces that are then filled with the molten bronze.

Obviously, both techniques are more complicated than this, but a verbal description alone without ample photographs and diagrams could tell little about these complex and involved processes.

MANDAMUS by George Kokis

STONEWARE

(Photograph by the artist)

MONO ANGULATED SURFACE IN SPACE by Max Bill, 1959

(Courtesy of the Detroit Institute of Arts)

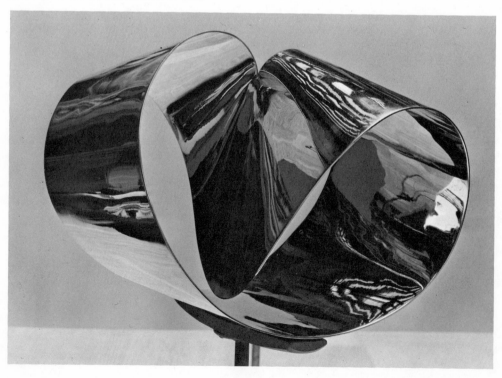

14

Contemporary Media and Techniques

In the twentieth century there is no aspect of man's life that has not been subjected to the sharp re-evaluation and modification brought about by the speed with which science and technology have been surging forward into the unknown. The "benefits" of this progress are already widespread though we do not yet fully understand what is happening to us, and our destiny is less certain than ever.

The art of our century has been sensitive to every discovery, invention and breakthrough that has occurred in the natural, social and physical sciences in the past century. Artists have reacted to this dynamic condition by creating revolutionary new forms supported by new aesthetics, at the same time embracing some of the residue of the near and distant past.

Andrew Ritchie, writing on the relationship of science and modern art says:

> Thus impressionism is unthinkable without the investigations of Helmholtz and other physicists into the properties of light. The post-impressionists, symbolists, and fauves, like Gauguin and Matisse, could not have investigated or been influenced by the primitive arts of Africa and Oceania without the previous researches and collections of nineteenth century ethnologists and anthropologists. And Cubism, likewise, was dependent upon ethnographic discoveries of primitive sculpture as well as new concepts in physics concerning the interdependence of space and time.

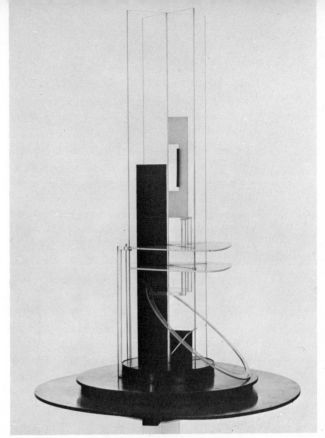

COLUMN by Naum Gabo, 1923

PLASTIC, WOOD, METAL

(Courtesy of the Solomon R. Guggenheim Museum)

Science and technology have provided us with new materials and techniques intended to serve the needs of industry and to accelerate the advances in pure and applied science. Artists have been quick to utilize these new tools and materials. Many of them have replaced the traditional studio equipment so that some studios look more like efficient laboratories or semi-automated machine shops.

The break with traditional art materials started with the Cubists who applied everyday, common materials to their paintings, collages and "inventions." Theater programs, newspaper clippings, string, wire, cloth, and wood affixed to the works heightened the tension between reality and its abstract representation. Umberto Boccioni in his *Manifesto of Futurist Sculpture,* published in 1912, advocated the use of "twenty different materials — glass, wood, cardboard, iron, cement, horsehair, leather, cloth, mirrors, electric lights, etc." In 1920 Naum Gabo published *The Realistic Manifesto,* later called the *Constructivist Manifesto,* in which he called for the use of new materials that made possible the creation of works concerned with space, time and movement rather than mass and volume. He also rejected the imitative role of sculpture and advocated the making of constructions that would not imitate anything found in nature. Sheets of translucent plastics and metal wire were used to make sculpture devoid of mass and volume.

Around 1930 welded metal as a medium for sculpture became important in the hands of Julio Gonzalez and Pablo Picasso. The welded iron and steel technique brought about a complete change in the *look* of sculpture and influenced a whole generation of sculptors, causing changes in their concepts of form and content. (This important contemporary medium is covered extensively in Part II of this book.)

Space-age materials have structural and plastic properties that appeal to imaginative sculptors. The superadhesives recently developed by the plastics industry permit the cementing together of almost any existing solids, while coatings of these resins can impart great permanence to the most fragile of substances. For example, papier mâché, a traditionally weak and impermanent material, becomes a practical sculpture medium if synthetic adhesives and coatings are used. The large number of thermosetting and thermo-plastic resins available are capable of exciting the imagination of any artist looking for new materials to work with. Polyester and epoxy resins, silicones, acrylics, and vinyls, polycarbonates, polyethylene, and cellulosics are some of these being used. (Fiberglass reinforced polyester resin is covered fully in Part III of this book.) The solid acrylics such as *Lucite* and *Plexiglas* are available in crystal-clear sheets and blocks. This material is easily formed, shaped, cut, and assembled in the studio without expensive equipment; much can be accomplished with heat lamps and simple hand tools. Because these thermoplastic resins are so easily worked and have effective optical qualities, they have been popular for some time with hobbyists and decorators. However, in spite of the carved, crystal-clear napkin rings, lamp bases, paper weights, and bookends, the solid acrylics have become an important sculpture medium.

To achieve the massive, volumetric

WOMAN COMBING HER HAIR
by Julio Gonzalez, 1936

WROUGHT IRON

(The Museum of Modern Art Collection, New York)

forms typical of traditional sculpture created in stone, wood or clay, but without the corresponding weight, the plastic foams seem most suitable. An additive causes gases to form in the rapidly gelling, catalyzed resin, and the resulting network of tiny cells imparts bulk and rigidity to the greatly expanded material. The foaming agent can produce up to thirty times more volume with no increase in weight. The foaming can be done in a mold, or the pre-foamed material is available in blocks that can be machined, carved or assembled. *Styrofoam* is the best known of these expanded materials.

Due to the fragility of foamed plastic, sculpture made with it is usually cast in 'a more durable substance such as aluminum. Foam is also used as a core to be coated with more durable reinforced plastics or cement.

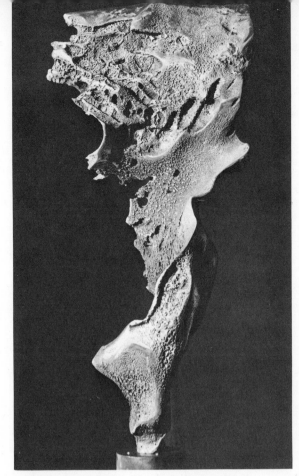

FLAME by Jan Zach

ALUMINUM CAST FROM FOAMED POLYETHYLENE

(Photograph by Ken McAllister)

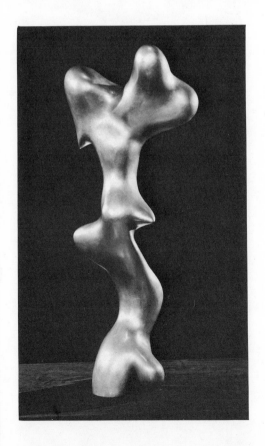

GROWTH by Jean Arp, 1938

BRONZE

(Courtesy of the Philadelphia Museum of Art)

17

CHAINED TURKEY POT by Jim Leedy

STONEWARE

(Courtesy of Mr. and Mrs. Clifford McCarthy. Photograph by Dave Base)

Some of the polyvinyl resins that are widely used in paints can be utilized for sculpture as coatings, binders and adhesives. Polyvinyl acetate and polyvinyl chloride are excellent adhesives and the latter is very stable out-of-doors. Fragile and impermanent materials such as paper, cloth, sawdust, and cardboard can be converted into permanent sculpture media if the polyvinyl resins are used in place of the old fashioned pastes, glues, paints, and varnishes. The acryloid resins also make excellent all-weather coatings for sculpture.

Other plastics that are not used directly for modeling, molding, casting, or hand forming can be utilized in the studio for the making of flexible molds, shell molds and mold separators. Plastic sheets are used for wrapping work in progress, either to keep moisture out or to seal it in and thus prevent rapid drying as in the case of modeling clay. Plastic foams provide excellent padding in shipping crates. Plastic-topped worktables and plastic skylights improve the

TORSO by Antoine Pevsner, 1924-26

PLASTIC AND COPPER

(The Museum of Modern Art Collection, New York. Katherine S. Dreier bequest)

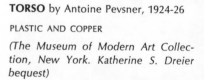

sculptor's work area—and, I might add, a plastic sandwich bag improves his lunch.

Sophisticated power tools with attachments for every purpose have also reduced some of the physical labor traditionally related to sculpture. However, despite the efficiency of these mechanical marvels, not all contemporary sculptors have been attracted to them. There are still many operations that can be performed only by hand, and some sculptors refuse to give up any of the direct, physical contact with their material for fear of becoming spiritually detached.

Some of the great sculpture of modern art has been created in the traditional way. Sculptors like Henry Moore Marino Marini, Alexander Archipenko, Jacques Lipchitz, Hans Arp, Constantin Brancusi and Alberto Giacometti have found no difficulty in creating new forms and images with the traditional materials and techniques of the carvers

Untitled Sculpture by William Stewart

CORK, FABRIC, WOOD, METAL, SYNTHETIC ADHESIVES

(Photograph by Doug Stewart)

ORGANIC FORM by James Pinto

BRONZE

(Photograph by Arturo Suarez)

CHELSEA REACH by Gabriel Kohn

LAMINATED WOOD

(Courtesy of the Marlborough-Gerson Gallery. Photograph by Rudolph Burckhardt)

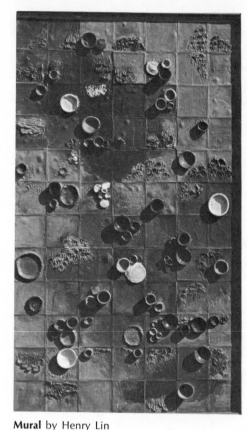

Mural by Henry Lin

CERAMIC

(Seigfred Hall, Ohio University. Photograph by Dana Vibberts)

POLITICAL PRISONER by George Goundie

WELDED STEEL

and modelers of the past. This is not as paradoxical as it might seem. In reacting against the banal and sentimental sculpture of the ninetenth century created by effete artists repelled by the arduous and messy problems of technique, these moderns, through a new spiritual and physical involvement with the materials of sculpture, revived the dignity of the art and the virility of the craft.

Many sculptors still use the traditional materials and techniques with modern variations and applications. In addition to using power tools to form the traditional stone and wood, some sculptors are carving synthetic materials such as cast stone, cast or laminated wood and plastics. Slow-setting synthetic resins mixed with metallic powders, wood chips, diatomaceous earths and other fillers are also modeled in the traditional way. *SculptMetal* is a popular medium of this type. Once cured, these resin-based modeling putties are hard and durable, needing no further processing to be made permanent. In this case modeling may be considered a *direct* method of producing sculpture.

Other artists still model with clay, wax and plaster in the traditional manner, but cast their sculpture in new materials such as alumina cement or clear and reinforced plastics. (See illustrations.) Variations on the traditional metal casting techniques are being developed at an accelerated pace. Styrofoam patterns, carved or molded, are being used to advantage. The styrofoam, being a greatly expanded plastic, vaporizes when the molten metal is poured into the mold or investment. This eliminates the need to remove the pattern, which is necessary when casting in sand or the lost-wax method. Ceramic shell investments permit a rapid burn-out of the wax pattern, allow for simpler venting systems and produce high fidelity reproductions of the original.

The advantages of these new materials and techniques over the traditional methods are greater speed and econ-

CHRYSALIS by Lily Landis

POWDERED ALUMINUM, EPOXY, GROUND BRASS DUST

(Photograph by Soichi Sunami)

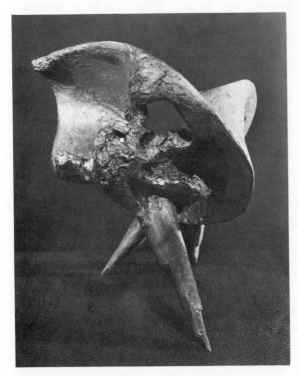

BRIDE OF THE MINOTAUR
by James Kearns

CAST FIBERGLASS

(Photograph by Oliver Baker)

21

omy, increased size and strength in relation to weight, accessibility of materials, the possibility of new forms, and the emotional satisfaction of working with the materials and technology of our time. Consequently many artists prefer to use them.

One example of a very sophisticated variation of an old technique is the experimental sculpture of Piotr Kowalski. His forms are blasted into shape by controlled underwater explosions. In effect he is accomplishing on a large scale and with one "blow" what artists have been doing for centuries — forming sheet metal by hammering.

With artists using materials as disparate as metal, clay, wood, glass, stone, and plastics, and forming them by welding, casting, gluing, spraying, sandblasting, carving, modeling, constructing, laminating, and even underwater bombing, it is inevitable that new and unfamiliar forms will be created. Novelty alone is insufficient justification for these art forms, but can we seriously challenge them with yesterday's aesthetics?

Sculpture by Piotr Kowalski

STAINLESS STEEL

The forms were achieved by an underwater explosive forming process used in industry.

(Courtesy of North American Aviation, Inc.)

FEAST OF CORPUS by John Baldwin

WELDED STEEL

(Photograph by Doug Stewart)

GLADIATOR by John Baldwin
WELDED STEEL
(Photograph by Doug Stewart)

PART II

WELDED METAL SCULPTURE:

A Twentieth-Century Revolution

THE OFFERING by John Baldwin

WELDED STEEL

(Collection of Mr. and Mrs. John Sprague, Michigan. Photograph by Doug Stewart)

Welding is the fusion of two pieces of the same metal by melting the adjoining edges and puddling or mixing them together to form a continuous, autogenous bond when cooled. Soldering is the joining of two pieces of like or unlike metal with another metal such as silver, brass or an alloy of lead and tin. When brass is used the process is called brazing.

Background

There is no disputing the powerful effect that welded metal has had on the development of recent modern sculpture. The technique had become almost universally accepted by the mid-fifties causing one critic to refer to that period as the "New Iron Age."

In 1927 Julio Gonzalez began to make welded iron sculpture. Gonzalez, coming from a family of goldsmiths in Barcelona, settled in Paris and learned the oxy-acetylene welding technique in the Renault factory during World War I. Around 1930 Pablo Picasso met Gonzalez and asked him for technical help with some metal constructions he was producing. Although both men were from Barcelona, they were at opposite poles in temperament and personality; in spite of this, each influenced the other to the extent that Gonzalez' new sculpture was decidedly more imaginative and abstract than before while Picasso's became more lyrical and refined. They each produced open, spatial constructions combining both linear and planar elements that animated space in a combination of the Cubist, Constructivist and Surrealist idioms.

In 1933 David Smith, influenced by reproductions of the metal sculpture of Gonzalez and Picasso, and impatient with the two-dimensional limitations of painting, borrowed some welding equipment and produced the first welded sculpture in America. Smith, excited by the medium, found that within its limitations and possibilities he could make "as complete a statement about form and color" as he wished. The emotional stimulation he received from working with steel was attested to when he wrote: "The metal possesses little art history. What associations it possesses are those of this century; power, structure, movement, progress, suspension, destruction, brutality."

Welding had the same explosive effect on modern sculpture that the oil medium had on painting in the fifteenth century. After the Second World War, welded sculpture proliferated at such a rate that sculpture rivaled the position of primacy held by painting for the first time since the Gothic era. Many painters replaced their brushes with the welding torch when they found that the technique was easy to learn, the tools and materials were accessible, and the total engagement demanded by the flaming torch and the molten metal was psychologically appealing. The searing sparks, the hiss of burning gases under high pressure, the protective clothing, and eye-saving goggles all provided the excitement and drama they had not found in painting. The medium also provided a technological link with our culture.

The direct and immediate results achieved with a puddle of molten metal, controlled and manipulated by a sharply pointed flame, suited the temperament of a generation of sculptors strongly influenced by Abstract Expressionism and Action Painting. While the "fast brush" dominated the painting of the late forties and fifties, the welding torch dominated sculpture.

History of Welding

The first practical welding equipment was developed around the turn of the century by Edmond Fouché in collaboration with a man named Picard. Since the thirteenth century, iron had been welded by heating it in a forge fired with charcoal or soft coal until it reached a white heat. The pieces to be joined were then hammered together on an anvil. In 1895 a French chemist named LeChatelier discovered that acetylene mixed with oxygen produced the hottest flame known since Prometheus stole fire from the gods (5300° — 6300°F). This discovery was followed by the development of cheap methods of manufacturing acetylene from calcium carbide. Oxygen was obtained by extracting it from liquified air. In a very few years the industrial applications of oxy-acetylene welding became widespread throughout Europe and by 1907 it was being tried successfully in the United States.

ROYAL BIRD by David Smith, 1948

STAINLESS STEEL

(Courtesy of the Walker Art Center, Minneapolis. T. B. Walker Foundation Acquisition)

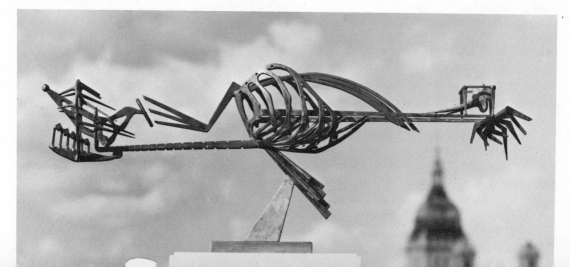

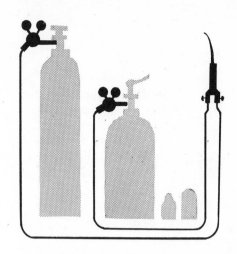

WELDING EQUIPMENT

The minimum welding equipment one must have to make direct-metal sculpture at first seems overwhelming. However, considering the amount of heavy equipment and tools usually found in a sculptor's studio, whether he models or carves, and also that this is a direct metal technique which eliminates the need for foundry casting, in itself requiring a great deal of heavy equipment, the welding apparatus used by the sculptor is not excessive.

Oxygen and Acetylene

To produce this hot flame that quickly reduces metal to a molten state it is necessary to have a controlled mixture of oxygen and acetylene at a constant working pressure. Oxygen and acetylene are stored separately in steel cylinders made to government specifications.

Because the nearly pure oxygen is stored at a pressure of approximately 2000 pounds per square inch, the cylinder is forged in one piece of high carbon steel. The acetylene cylinder is usually shorter and wider than the oxygen cylinder and for reasons of safety the interior consists of a pulpy substance saturated with acetone. The acetylene is dissolved into the acetone under a pressure of about 250 pounds per square inch.

These cylinders should always be treated with care and stored in an upright position with the valve closed, whether they are empty or full. A safety chain should always secure the cylinders in a portable cart or against some fixed, stable support. The oxygen valve is fitted with a pressure safety-device and is called a back-seating valve. When the valve is in the full, open position, the stem seals itself to prevent leakage. Oxygen leaking under such high pressure would burn anything it touched and the cylinder would become a veritable rocket. The valve caps should always be screwed in place over the valves when the cylinders are being transported.

Acetylene cylinders are equipped with safety plugs that will melt and relieve the internal pressure at temperatures above 165°F. The valve stem should be tested for leakage occasionally with soapy water, and if any is found, it should be corrected immediately by tightening the packing nut or replacing the cylinder. Acetylene is highly explosive when mixed with the air in an enclosed space. Always work with the acetylene valve open only about one turn and with the "T"-wrench in place so that it may be quickly shut down in case of an emergency.

Regulators and Gauges

As the pressures under which the oxygen and acetylene are stored in the cylinders far exceed the normal working pressures at the torch (only up to 30 pounds per square inch, some method of reducing the pressures and keeping them constant must be employed. Two pressure regulators are used for this purpose.

The principle behind regulating gas pressure and keeping it constant is relatively simple. A flexible diaphragm mounted between springs provides a compensating action that permits only that volume of gas determined by the setting of the adjusting screw to pass from the tank to the torch. When the gas flows through the torch, the pressure inside the regulator drops, permitting the springs, depressed by the adjusting screw, to move the diaphragm sufficiently to open the tiny orifice through which more gas will enter from the cylinder. Immediately the pressure inside the regulator increases, forcing the diaphragm back and again closing off the orifice. This compensating action is so smooth that a constant working pressure is maintained at whatever

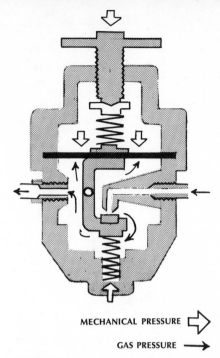

MECHANICAL PRESSURE ▷

GAS PRESSURE ⟶

DIAGRAM 1. Gas Pressure Regulator

setting the operator requires. (Diagram 1.) Each regulator is equipped with two gauges. The high-pressure gauge connected between the cylinder valve and the regulator indicates the pressure in the cylinder and tells when it is full or empty. The low-pressure gauge, connected to the diaphragm chamber, indicates the working pressure of the gas. (Diagram 2.)

DIAGRAM 2. Oxygen Gauges — Acetylene Gauges

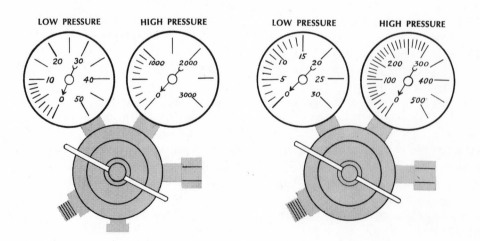

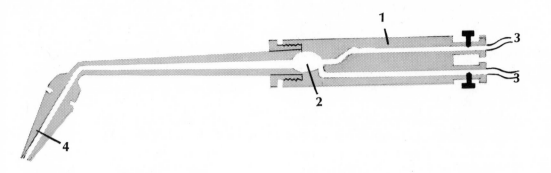

DIAGRAM 3. Welding Torch
1. Barrel **2.** Mixing Chamber **3.** Oxygen and Acetylene Valves **4.** Tip

Hoses

The oxygen and acetylene are carried from the regulators to the torch through separate reinforced rubber hoses. These hoses are connected to the regulators and the torch by means of brass nuts fastened to the ends of the hose. To prevent the connecting of the acetylene hose to the oxygen regulator, or the oxygen hose to the acetylene regulator, three safety devices are used. First, the hoses are color coded. The acetylene hose is red and the oxygen hose is green. Second, the nuts are marked OXY and ACE and the acetylene nut is grooved. Third, the most foolproof safety device is the use of left-hand threads on the acetylene regulator, hose and torch connections. Oxygen connections have the normal right-hand threads.

The Torch

The welding torch is that part of the equipment held in the hand and manipulated by the artist when creating welded sculpture. Like any hand tool, the artist must get the "feel" of it. It should be of a size and type that fits his hand and is suitable to work being undertaken. There are several types of torches and they come in various sizes. Some are quite small and light, not much larger than a felt-tip drawing pen. Others are as big and round as the small end of a baseball bat. The larger, heavy-duty torches are more expensive and designed to take more abuse. However, I have found the small and medium size torches more useful for making sculpture of moderate size and complexity of form where dexterity and facility of movement is most necessary.

The torch (Diagram 3) consists of (1) a barrel or cylindrical body; (2) a mixing chamber inside of the barrel where the two gases are mixed; (3) a set of valves to turn on, shut off and adjust the flow of the two gases, and (4) a tip at the end of a tube where the combustion takes place.

The cutting torch is essentially the same as a welding torch. There is an extra oxygen valve and an extra orifice in the tip which permits a jet of pure oxygen to be played on the pre-heated metal. (The use of oxy-acetylene cutting equipment is discussed later.)

Welding Tips

Welding tips come with different size orifices numbered from 0 to 15 and the size of the tip used depends upon the gauge of the metal being welded. The oxygen and acetylene pressures should be adjusted as recommended by the manufacturer of your particular welding equipment.

Welding and cutting tips are made of a hard copper and should be treated with care to insure the best results. Never tighten them with a pair of pliers as the teeth will chew up the copper. Always use an open-end wrench of the proper size. Tighten but do not force the tip to avoid ruining the seat. No welding equipment connections should ever be forced or over-tightened. The tip should never touch the metal being welded and, if the orifice should become dirty or clogged, ream it with a special tip reamer of the correct diameter. Since a large portion of the oxygen utilized in welding comes from the air adjacent to the flame, the tip should be kept free of carbon and other encrustations to prevent turbulence and to permit a smooth flow of air to the flame. Wipe the tip occasionally on a piece of leather or a block of wood.

Most of this equipment can be purchased in kits that provide the beginner with everything essential for welding, brazing and cutting. The cylinders are usually rented from a supplier of oxygen and acetylene gases. Before purchasing any welding equipment, one should shop around to compare the quality and the prices.

The Shop

Besides the welding equipment, it is necessary to have a welding table. Basically this is a table with a steel frame and a metal or fire-brick top. Never weld on a wood surface as it will burn, and cement or stone surfaces will shatter and send small pieces flying.

The room should be as fireproof as possible. Always weld on an earth, brick stone, or cement floor. If it is wood, it should be protected with sand, metal or asbestos sheets. All flammable materials should be removed from the area for a distance of at least 30 feet since sparks from the work can jump that distance. If it is not possible to clear that distance, a metal or asbestos screen should be constructed around the welding area. Always check the local fire regulations before setting up your equipment.

SENTINELS by John Baldwin

WELDED COPPER

(Art Institute of Zanesville Collection. Photograph by Doug Stewart)

Equipment: 1. Acetylene Tank **2.** Oxygen Tank **3.** Acetylene Regulator and Gauges **4.** Oxygen Regulator and Gauges **5.** Acetylene Valve **6.** Oxygen Valve **7.** Chain for Securing Tanks **8.** Hoses **9.** Torch **10.** Flint Striker **11.** Leather Glove **12.** Welding Goggles

(Photograph by the author)

SETTING UP YOUR EQUIPMENT

The following procedure should be followed in setting up the welding equipment:

1. Secure the cylinders to a portable cart or to the wall, a post, or a work bench with a chain so they cannot fall over.

2. Take-off the cylinder caps protecting the valves, stand to one side and, one at a time, open and shut the valves sufficiently to blow any dust out of the valve seat.

3. Connect the regulators to the cylinders with an open-end wrench. Do not force. The acetylene regulator has a left-hand thread. Stand aside and check the pressure in each cylinder, one at a time, by opening the cylinder valve slowly until full pressure registers on the high-pressure gauge. The oxygen cylinder valve should be opened all the way. The acetylene valve only about one turn—leave the acetylene wrench in place for an emergency shut-off.

4. Connect the hoses to the regulators and the torch. The green hose is for the oxygen and the red hose (with

left-hand threads) is for the acetylene. Tighten with an open-end wrench and, again, do not use force.

5. Attach the torch tube and proper tip to the barrel.

6. Adjust the working pressure by first opening the oxygen valve on the torch a half turn. Then turn the regulator adjusting screw slowly to the right. The pressure will show on the low-pressure oxygen gauge and it will increase as you continue to turn the screw to the right. Stop at the pressure specified for the tip size being used. Now close the torch valve. Open the acetylene torch valve a half turn and follow the same procedure.

With all of the equipment connected and both cylinder valves open, and the working pressure adjusted as indicated on each low-pressure gauge, you are now ready to start welding.

Shutting Down Your Equipment

If you are interrupting your work for only a few minutes, it is enough to close the torch valves and set it aside. However, if you plan to leave the equipment for a longer time, it is good practice to completely shut down the station. To do this, follow these steps:

1. Extinguish the torch in the usual way by closing the acetylene valve first and then the oxygen valve.

2. Close both cylinder valves tightly.

3. Open the torch valves to drain the lines.

4. When both the acetylene and oxygen high- and low-pressure gauges register zero, back out the adjusting screws on both regulators (counter clockwise) until loose.

5. Close the hand valves on the torch.

Checking for Leaks

When the equipment is set up for the first time, and periodically thereafter, a thorough check should be made for leaks. Leaks anywhere in the line can be costly and dangerous. Using a clean brush and greaseless soapy water, test each connection and valve stem from the cylinders to the tip of the torch. Check each line separately with the valves open and one finger over the orifice in the tip. If there is a leak, it will be indicated by the appearance of soap bubbles. Correct all leaks before starting to weld.

SANTO by John Baldwin

WELDED STEEL, COPPER AND BRONZE

(Photograph by Doug Stewart)

WOMAN by Pat Kelly

WELDED SHEET METAL

(Photograph by Doug Stewart)

ARMORED HORSE by John Baldwin

WELDED STEEL

(Photograph by Doug Stewart)

Carburizing

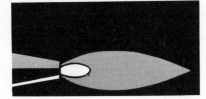

Neutral

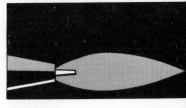

Oxidizing

THE FLAME

The welding flame must be clean and controlled to insure the application of a very intense heat to a very small area. If the flame is not properly adjusted, too much carbon or too much oxygen will spoil the weld. When the mixture of oxygen and acetylene is correct, the flame is neutral—the oxygen is just sufficient to burn out the carbon and hydrogen in the acetylene, creating the maximum heat (about 6000°F) with no harmful by-products. A good welding flame should be hot enough to melt the metals and be continuous to make up for the heat lost through radiation, convection and conduction. It should also be clean and free from impurities including carbon.

Igniting and Adjusting the Flame

With the gauges set at the correct pressure for the tip size and thickness of metal being welded (as recommended by the manufacturer of your equipment), open the acetylene torch-valve about ¼ turn. Ignite the acetylene at the end of the tip with a flint striker. (A lighted candle near the welding stand is sometimes preferred as one's hands are often too occupied holding the torch, welding rod, and the work, to operate the striker.) You will notice that the acetylene burns with a bright yellow flame and produces a lot of black smoke. (Diagram 4A.) Open the acetylene valve farther until the flame jumps slightly away from the tip. (Diagram 4B.) Now gently open the oxygen valve on the torch. As the amount of oxygen is increased, the bright yellow acetylene flame becomes smaller and turns blue. (Diagram 4C.) A small inner

cone with a sharp contour will appear and, at the point where the yellowish acetylene "feather" disappears and the inner cone becomes sharp, the adjustment is correct. This is a neutral flame and the one recommended. (Diagram 4D.) If the flame remains large and yellow, too much acetylene is being used and a "carburizing" or "reducing" flame is being produced. If the small, blue flame continues to shrink after the outer "feather" disappears and there is a very sharp, blue flame with a lot of hissing, too much oxygen is being used. (Diagram 4E.) An oxydizing flame may burn the metal being welded.

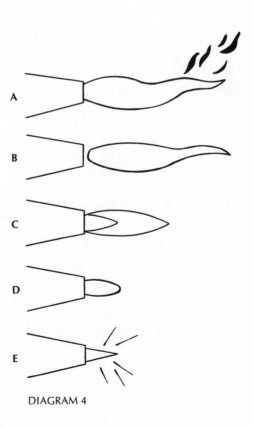

DIAGRAM 4

To extinguish the flame, the acetylene valve on the torch should be closed first, and then the oxygen valve. This avoids the black smoke and soot that is produced by burning pure acetylene. It also eliminates the loud popping sound that results when the oxygen is turned off first.

EXERCISE I—
PRACTICE WITH THE TORCH

Unlike welders in industry who have to lay down miles of molten metal in a uniform and prescribed way according to established specifications for the material being used, the sculptor who uses the oxy-acetylene flame to achieve his own unique forms has few restrictions or restraints as to what may or may not be done. You may experience some technical limitations in the beginning and there may be some fear and apprehension, but all this passes after a few hours of practice with the torch.

Beginning to Weld

First to be developed is coordination and facility in guiding the torch and the welding rod along the joins and into those places where the welding is to be done. Lighting and adjusting the flame, remembering to pull the goggles over your eyes, finding the welding rod and tools in the dimmed light, locating the place to be welded, supporting the pieces temporarily, keeping the flame the correct distance from the weld, and freeing the rod every time it gets stuck in the cooling puddle, are some of the activities that will require repeated practice if you are to perform efficiently. Until a beginner has mistakenly picked up the hot end of a welding rod in his bare hand, establishing good work habits may seem unimportant. There is a tendency among beginners

Student Welding

(Photograph by the author)

FIGURE 1

(Photograph by Doug Stewart)

to "hurry up and make sculpture" before even a minimum of skill is acquired.

Here is a simple exercise that will help develop some co-ordination and sensitivity in aiming the torch and welding rod and will also provide practice in lighting and extinguishing the flame. First cut some welding rods of different thicknesses into varying lengths. Practice joining these rods end-to-end without burning the metal and without allowing the puddled metal to run and drip before the join is made. After several pieces are successfully joined, try joining the end of one piece of rod to the length of another at right angles to it. (Figure 1.) Use a fire-brick for support and aim the flame so that one rod is not repeatedly burned in two. When you have accomplished this many times and all the welds withstand testing, place several rods on the fire-brick parallel so they touch. Spot weld the pieces together by fusing the parallel rods about every inch with a drop of metal from a filler rod slightly thinner than the rods being joined. You will notice a certain amount of warping in the rods. This can be minimized by preheating the metal an inch or two around the place where you intend to weld. Overheating in one spot can be avoided by distributing the spot welds in a random pattern rather than progressing along one rod at a time. This allows the welds to cool and ties all the rods into a network that reinforces itself against warping.

Once the control and skill necessary to perform these simple welds is developed and you feel more confidence in handling the equipment, try making a simple structure out of rods. Don't be too concerned with the design. Let the form develop naturally. Concentrate primarily on handling the torch and the rod. Make several of these little constructions. You will find the time has been well spent when you undertake a larger project.

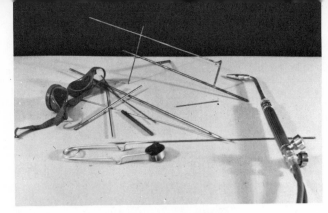

FIGURE 2

(Photograph by the author)

Student Sculpture

(Photograph by the author)

MOUNTED HOST
by John Baldwin

WELDED STEEL RODS

*(Mr. and Mrs. Cooper Campbell
Collection, Toronto, Canada)*

CIRCUS by John Baldwin

BRAZED WELDING ROD—KINETIC

*(Lorenza Story Collection,
San Miguel Allende, Mexico)*

Sculpture with Rods

The welded sculpture shown on these two pages was made primarily with lengths of welding rod.

CENTURIAN by John Baldwin

WELDED STEEL RODS

*(Mr. and Mrs. Verne Offerman
Collection, McAllen, Texas)*

BIRD OF PREY by John Baldwin

WELDED STEEL RODS

*(Mr. and Mrs. Max Lutz
Collection, McAllen, Texas)*

MARTIAN by George Goundie

BRAZED WELDING ROD

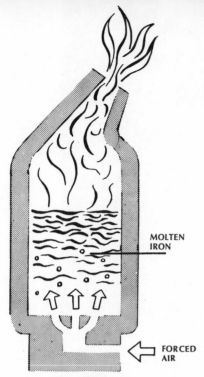

MOLTEN IRON

FORCED AIR

Bessemer Furnace

FERROUS METALS

Most of the ferrous and non-ferrous metals are the materials used in making sculpture with the oxy-acetylene torch. The ferrous metals are those that contain only iron and a little carbon. The non-ferrous metals contain no iron.

Iron is mined as a crumbly, red earth. This iron ore must be heated to a high temperature in a blast furnace to extract the usable metal. The ore is heated on a bed of coals through which a blast of air is forced. As the temperature increases, the impurities and some carbon are burned off, the iron ore is deoxidized, and the iron and flux (limestone) become molten. The slag (dirt and impurities) is floated off by the molten flux, leaving the slightly carbonized, molten iron to be tapped from the bottom of the furnace. This pig iron, as it is called, is usually further refined in several different kinds of furnaces, each

producing an iron or steel of special qualities.

The carbon content in iron determines its quality and usefulness. An increase in the carbon content makes iron harder but also more brittle and less malleable. Through heat treatments and by alloying iron with other metals, the manufacturers of steel attempt to obtain those qualities most desirable for a particular use.

Wrought Iron and Steel

Wrought iron and mild steel are the metals most widely used by sculptors because they weld easily. They contain the smallest amounts of carbon (.003 and .15 respectively) which makes them very malleable, soft and, at the same time, tough. Wrought iron is rust resistant and widely used for ornamental and structural work. Iron containing about .10 to 2.0 percent carbon is classified as steel. It is used commercially for innumerable items such as nails, screws and bolts to the most sophisticated and intricate machinery and tools.

Alloy Steels

An alloy is an intimate mixture of two or more metals that do not separate into layers upon cooling. The most common metals alloyed with steel are chromium, nickel, silicon, molybdenum, tungsten, vanadium, titanium, and copper. Stainless steel is an alloy of chromium nickel and carbon steel. It has a high resistance to corrosion as well as a bright color and lustre. Stainless steels must be welded with care or the corrosion-resistance of the metal will be destroyed. Special flux and rods are necessary, and a slightly carburizing flame from a tip one size smaller than that used for plain steel is recommended. The metal should be puddled or stirred as little as possible and the flame should be aimed at approximately an 80° angle to the surface. Some alloy steels require an immediate, complicated heat treatment with special equipment not always available to the sculptor.

Impurities

Some metals are less suited for welding than others. Impurities in steel, most commonly phosphorus and sulphur, make welding difficult and often result in a poor job. The industry therefore tries to keep these impurities below .05 percent. Impurities will cause excessive sparks and sputtering while welding because of the formation of gas in the molten metal. Holes result in the finished weld when the metal boils and bubbles. During the rolling process or some other mechanical working of the metal, dirt or slag (iron oxide) may become imbedded in the steel. If a high percentage of this slag or dirt is present, poor welds will result. The metal will not fuse easily and the welds will appear burned and pitted.

Before welding it is a good practice to test the metal to be used. This is done by playing a neutral flame on one spot of the metal to form a puddle. The amount of sparks should not be excessive and the puddle should be molten but not boiling. The surface tension should permit the molten metal to flow as directed by the torch and, when cool, the surface of the puddle should be smooth, blue-black and shiny. It should not be pitted or discolored.

Miscellaneous Ferrous Metals

For steels with a high carbon content (above 70 point carbon) bronze soldering (brazing) is recommended instead of fusion welding. White and grey cast iron can be fusion-welded but malleable iron should be brazed. Galvanized iron or steel may be brazed or welded but the toxic white fumes that result from the burning of the zinc coating should not be inhaled. Always work in a well-ventilated place.

CIRCLE OF TACTILITY by Fred Pallini

WELDED STEEL

(Stephen Micola Collection. Photograph by Doug Stewart)

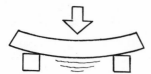

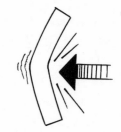

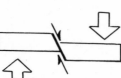 

Mechanical Properties of Materials

1. *Flexural Strength:* The ability to bend under load and return to its original state when the load is removed, providing the elastic limit is not exceeded.
2. *Tensile Strength:* Amount of pulling force a material can withstand before tearing or separating — opposite of compression.
3. *Compressive Strength:* The amount of pressure a material can withstand before bursting, buckling or shearing. It is the opposite of tensile strength.
4. *Shear Strength:* The ability to withstand equal and opposite forces tangential to an imaginary plane.
5. *Impact Strength:* The ability to withstand sudden loads such as a blow with a hammer.
6. *Hardness:* The ability to withstand penetration, indentation or scratching from load pressure, blows or friction.
7. *Brittleness:* Quality of breaking suddenly after very little tensile strain.
8. *Malleability:* Ability to be worked or formed into various shapes without breaking or returning to its original shape.
9. *Ductility:* The ability to withstand high tensile strain before breaking.

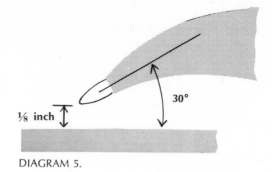

1/8 inch

30°

DIAGRAM 5.

EXERCISE II

Having joined pieces of rod together in the previous exercises, you should feel less apprehensive about handling a 6,000°F flame and be a little more nimble with the torch and rod. To the beginner, the first session with the welding torch is a real baptism of fire.

Puddling and Welding a Bead

The most important thing a welder must learn is to form a puddle of molten metal and move that puddle along the part to be welded, forming a bead. This bead should be clean, glossy and rippled, not bumpy or pitted. Its width and penetration should be consistent with the thickness of the metal being welded and there should be no holes burned clear through the parent metal. For better results, it is a good practice to heat a one- or two-inch area around the weld to a dull red before starting to form a puddle. By slowly bringing the metal to a molten temperature, the internal stresses and strains are relieved.

With a small piece of 16-gauge sheet steel on the welding stand, a number three tip attached to the torch, and the oxygen and acetylene pressure adjusted to about three pounds each, light up the torch and adjust the welding goggles over your eyes. With the flame properly adjusted, hold the tip of the inner cone $\frac{1}{16}$ inch to $\frac{1}{8}$ inch from the surface of the metal and aimed approximately at a 30° angle to it until a puddle

of molten metal is formed. (Diagram 5.) Move the puddle along in the same direction the torch tip is pointing by slightly adjusting the angle of the flame. You will notice that the pressure of the burning gases pushes the molten metal forward and out to the sides while the bead tends to sag. Because of this, a filler rod (welding rod) is used to add metal and make the bead stronger.

FIGURE 3. Welding a bead.

(Photograph by Doug Stewart)

Choose a welding rod that has a diameter the same as, or smaller than, the thickness of the metal being welded. Hold the tip of the rod about ⅜ inch from the inner cone of the flame and about ⅛ inch above the puddle. When it is white hot, dip the rod into the molten puddle where it will melt, then lift it out to its previous position in relation to the flame and puddle. Practice this a few times. The tip of the rod should never be allowed to cool or it will stick when re-inserted into the puddle and it should never be allowed to get so hot that it oxidizes or drips molten metal into the puddle. The only time the rod should melt is when it is in the puddle.

Now practice welding a bead by moving the puddle and inserting the filler rod in a continuous rhythmic motion of the torch and the rod. The motion of the torch can be circular, oval or zigzag across the line of the weld and, at the same time, it should move slightly up and down. The movement should never carry the flame outside the limits of the puddle. With this co-ordinated movement of the rod and the torch, the bead progresses smoothly at a rate consistent with the rate of puddle formation. (Figure 3.)

Up to now the flame has been aimed in the same direction that the bead is progressing. This serves to preheat the metal as the heat is deflected ahead. For heavy gauge metal a back-hand weld is sometimes used. The flame is aimed back toward the metal already welded. This tends to anneal the weld, relieving some of the stress and strain caused by too rapid cooling, and also permits the puddle to make a deeper penetration of the weld. (Diagrams 6 and 7.)

DIAGRAM 6. Forward Weld

DIAGRAM 7. Backhand Weld

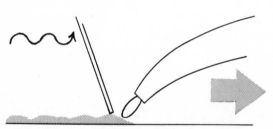

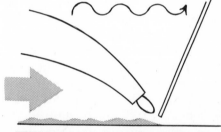

ARMORED HORSE (detail) by John Baldwin
(Photograph by Doug Stewart)

MECHANICAL DOG by Lothan Kestenbaum

WELDED STEEL

Welded Sculpture by Neil Cogbill

STEEL

(Photograph by the artist)

FIGURE 4. Welding an outside corner.

(Photograph by Doug Stewart)

Basic Welds

There are a few basic welds for joining two or more pieces contiguously. The peculiarities of each kind of weld will become apparent as you try joining the two pieces together. Practice will eliminate clumsiness and the resulting imperfect welds. Be certain to have the proper flame adjustment (neutral or very slightly carburizing), and use a co-ordinated, continuous, rythmic movement of torch and rod.

Butt Weld

The butt weld consists of joining the edges of two pieces of metal lying side by side in the same plane. The weld should penetrate to the underside and the edges as well as the center of the bead. It should be completely fused with the surface metal. When making a long butt weld it is sometimes better to spot-weld at several places to prevent the two pieces from separating because of distortions from the heat.

Inside Corner Weld

It is necessary to use an inside corner weld on some "L" joins and inverted "T" joins. The torch is directed into the corner, and because of the restricted circulation of the air, a heavy carburizing flame may result. To control this, slightly open the oxygen valve on the torch. Avoid undercutting the vertical piece of metal, and be certain that the fusion takes place at the base of the joint.

Lap Weld

The lap weld is easily accomplished if the edge of the top piece is thought of as a very small inside corner. Fill the "step" and build up a slight crown. The top piece will heat up faster than the bottom, so direct the flame more toward the bottom piece.

Outside Corner Weld

An outside corner is sometimes welded without the use of filler rod. The angle of the two pieces being joined forms a point that melts down, thus forming its own filler. If a clean, sharp angle is desired, however, filler rod may be used and the corner may be ground square.

Vertical Weld

For a vertical weld, aim the torch at a 15° to 30° angle. The pressure and velocity of the flame will support the molten metal and keep it from running and dripping. For a horizontal weld on a vertical surface, aim the torch at a slightly upward angle.

Overhead Weld

An overhead weld is the most difficult to make. Avoid standing under the work in progress as molten metal may drop and cause serious burns. Be certain to wear gauntlet-type gloves covering the ends of the sleeves. If at all possible, turn the work upside down or on its side.

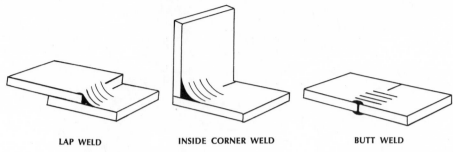

LAP WELD   INSIDE CORNER WELD   BUTT WELD

Backfire

During the welding process there may be a considerable amount of popping that sounds very much like a shooting gallery, accompanied by sparks and molten metal flying in all directions. This is caused by one or more of the following conditions and should be corrected as indicated to insure better welds and relieve wear and tear on the nerves.

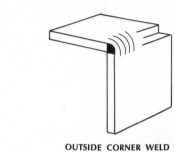

OUTSIDE CORNER WELD

DIAGRAM 8. Basic Welds.

1. *Pre-ignition*—caused by using too little gas pressure for the size of the orifice in the tip. Adjust the pressure of the oxygen and acetylene or use a smaller tip size.

2. *An overheated tip*—the result of being held too close to the puddle, or from too long and continuous use, or from working in an inside corner. To stop the popping, cool the tip.

3. *A clogged tip*—due to tiny pieces of carbon, metal or other dirt. Clean the orifice with the proper size cleaner wire and continue welding.

4. *The inner cone of the flame is too close to the puddle*—more practice is needed.

The welding bead created by a sculptor need not compare with standards set up for industrial welding and those possibly achieved in an industrial art course. However, the sculptor should

be able to operate the welding equipment and manipulate the torch so that his creative impulses are not thwarted by inadequate technique. The kind of bead he welds may express his personality but it must also hold the sculpture together. Good welds do not destroy the spontaneity of work and bad welds have never made a poor piece of sculpture better.

When you have practiced making the basic welds, and the rod is sticking less with the popping down to a minimum, try making some simple forms out of several pieces of light gauge steel like the student work reproduced on the next page.

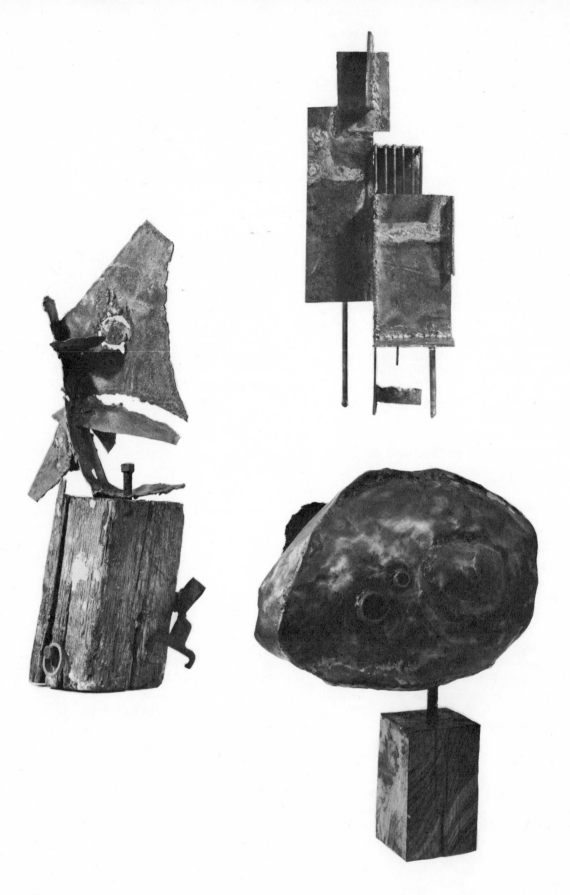

1. Following an enlarged pattern based on the mackerel's head, a piece of sheet metal was cut and peened to form a rudimentary head for the sculpture.

SMOKED AND WELDED GILLS

When sheet metal is cut to shape and bent to the desired form, it provides surface and volume quickly. Steel rods and wires of varying lengths and gauges connect the pieces of sheet metal and activate the space through and around the forms. They also function as an armature. Heavy gauge wire-mesh provides an interesting open texture. This, combined with the burned, dripped and puddled textures inherent in the welding technique, can add a rich tactility to the whole assembly.

While contemplating these formal possibilities of welded metal technique and simultaneously enjoying the flavor of a good smoked mackerel I had just eaten—the head of which I was studying with some fascination—I suddenly realized how well the fish form would lend itself to welded sculpture. The following series of photographs shows the result of these musings.

2. Several crescents were cut from the sheet metal with the welding torch. Light-gauge sheet steel can be cut with the welding torch instead of the cutting torch. (See Flame-cutting, page 52)

3. The "head," crescent shapes and a piece of hardware cloth from an old tractor were combined with some rods in different arrangements. Finally a fishlike structure began to develop.

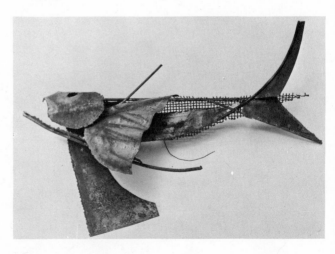

4. *Left*. After some internal braces were added, the entire form was studied from all sides. Chalk was used to mark changes and characteristic "features" that needed development. A ¼ inch rod was welded along these chalk lines to build up the surface forms three-dimensionally and to add strength to the sheet metal.

5. *Below*. The contour of each form was further developed by puddling the sheet metal along the edges until the desired shape was achieved. This was like *drawing* with the torch.

Opposite Page

6. *Above*. When the fins, gills and tail were shaped with the torch, they were braced with a network of ⅛ inch welding rods. Anything that was not connected at both ends or on all sides was braced in this way to minimize warping. Now the entire surface of the fish, inside and out, was covered with molten steel. The molten metal was spotted over all the forms in such a way as to eliminate all joints and connections, giving the illusion of one continuous molded surface.

7. *Below*. A steel base was designed to provide adequate support, since all of the weight was balanced on only one point. After a thorough cleaning with wire and bristle brushes (no water or solvents were used), the new sculpture was coated with several brushings of a sealer with a tungoil base, *Waterlox*.

This fish will never swim. It's not like any fish I have ever seen, but everytime I look at it I remember how delicious that mackerel really was.

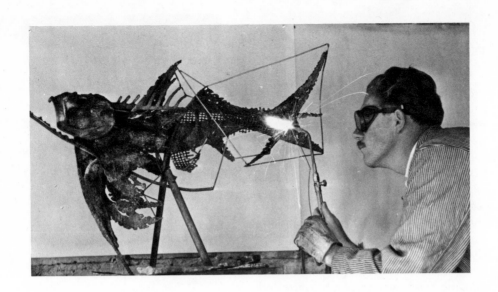

OF ANCIENT SEAS by John Baldwin

WELDED STEEL

(*Photograph by Doug Stewart*)

FLAME-CUTTING

Cutting metal with an oxy-acetylene torch or attachment is accomplished by preheating the metal almost to its melting point and then directing a jet of oxygen to where the cut is to be made. In effect, this is an accelerated rusting; iron oxide melts off as slag, continually exposing a fresh surface to the jet of oxygen. The pressure of the oxygen should be adjusted so that the molten slag is blown away as fast as it is produced. The resulting cut or kerf is straight and clean if the oxygen pressure and the torch are properly controlled. Metal from 1/16 inch to four feet thick can be cut with the oxy-acetylene flame.

The cutting torch or attachment has a cutting-oxygen lever, Diagram 9 (A) and an extra oxygen tube (B) that bypasses the mixing chamber (C). The cutting tip consists of a center orifice (D) connected directly to the oxygen tube, and smaller orifices (E) that surround the center one and are connected to the tube from the mixing chamber.

Before cutting metal, the oxygen pressure should be adjusted on the regulator to correspond to the size of cutting tip being used and to the thickness of the metal to be cut. These pressures will vary slightly depending on the manufacturer's specifications for a particular cutting tip. This increase in pressure can range from two to five times the pressure used for welding.

The oxy-acetylene preheating flame is ignited and adjusted in the same manner as a welding flame. The tip of the flame is held about 1/16 inch from the metal and aimed perpendicularly to the surface until the metal begins to melt. The cutting-oxygen valve should now be opened by pressing down on the lever. As the oxygen begins to cut there will be a shower of sparks. The torch should be tilted slightly in the direction of the cut. If the torch is moved too quickly the cutting will stop. Release

FIGURE 5.

1. SEATED WOMAN by John Baldwin

WELDED COPPER

(Mr. and Mrs. Charles Allen Smart Collection, Chillicothe, Ohio. Photograph by Doug Stewart)

2. Untitled Construction by James Pinto

WELDED STEEL PAINTED WITH ACRYLICS

(Photograph by Stirling Dickinson)

3. CRUSADER by John Baldwin

WELDED STEEL BRAZED WITH BRONZE

(Mr. and Mrs. George Cannata Collection, Hollywood, California. Photograph by the author)

4. FOUNTAIN SCULPTURE by Ted Egri

WELDED SHEET BRASS

(Courtesy of Dr. Rudolf Kieve, Santa Fe, New Mexico. Photograph by Joe Laval)

5. YELLOW AND BLACK by a student, Ohio University

WELDED STEEL PAINTED WITH ENAMEL

(Photograph by the author)

6. ENACTMENT by Ibram Lassaw

WELDED STEEL, VARIOUS BRONZE ALLOYS AND NICKEL SILVER

(Mr. and Mrs. Howard Lipman Collection, New York)

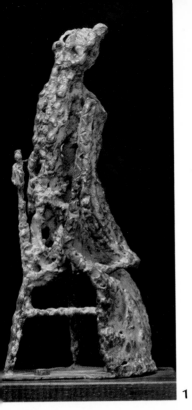

1

2

3

4

5

6

53

the lever and begin again from that point. If the oxygen pressure adjustment is correct and the torch is held at the proper distance and angle, and if it is moved along at the right speed, you should have no trouble flame-cutting metal.

For small cuts in light gauge metal you can use the welding torch. To do this, preheat the area to be cut; then when the metal begins to melt, quickly turn off the acetylene valve and open up the oxygen valve on the torch. This will not produce as clean a cut as one made with the cutting equipment, but for work where a rough edge is not objectionable (in sculpture it is often desirable), this method works.

Flame-cutting always produces a shower of sparks. Extra care must be taken to avoid fires and injury to yourself.

DIAGRAM 9. Cutting Torch

MACHINE PACIFIQUE by Robert Jacobsen

WELDED IRON

(Courtesy of the Galerie de France, Paris. Photograph by Pierre Joly — Vera Cardot)

THE METALLIC LOOK— FORMAL CHARACTERISTICS

The variety of shapes into which metals are cast, rolled, forged, extruded, and drawn is determined by the needs of industry and those engineering standards that demand a maximum of structural efficiency.

Sculptors who are Purists by nature and Constructivists by choice employ these forms in their metal sculpture without disguising them. Alan Bowness in his book, *Modern Sculpture*, says, "The twentieth-century sculptor need no longer disguise the fact that works of sculpture are made out of something —on the contrary, it becomes a point of honour not to conceal the fact that the sculpture is also a piece of wood or stone or cast metal or an assemblage of iron bars." When sections of "I" beam and channel iron are welded to sheets, plates, and rods, the resulting overall spatial configurations are powerfully evocative, symbolic and decidedly expressive of more than the raw material from which they are made. David Smith's work and the steel sculptures of Anthony Caro and others exemplify this approach to welded steel sculpture.

The tensile and flexural strength of a metal as well as its rigidity permit the spanning of considerable distances through space by relatively thin forms. Rods, tubes, heavy wire, and thin structural elements may be bent and twisted linearly through space, resulting in the open, spiky, fragmented forms typical of much welded sculpture. Sheets and plates are capable of planar convolutions creating the illusion of movement and weightlessness, or they may slice space into a complex of beautifully composed architectonic segments. Sheets may also be bent by hammering and then welded together to form a continuous closed "skin" typical of traditional mass-volume sculpture.

Variations and combinations of these "typical" ways of working with metal are capable of producing endless varieties of form so that no artist need feel that he has reached a dead end due to the limitations of the medium.

Welding techniques make the cutting, shaping, forming, and texturing of metals almost as plastic as modeling. The sculptors Theodore Roszak, Seymore Lipton ibram Lassaw, and Herbert Ferber were among the first to produce organic forms directly in metal that emanated a vitality, an aliveness not unlike that of a sentient, living organism. A critic attributed to these sculptors the credit for having solved the problem of how to make a welded, metal sculpture without being a Constructivist.

SPECTRE OF KITTY HAWK by Theodore J. Roszak

WELDED AND HAMMERED STEEL BRAZED WITH BRONZE AND BRASS

(The Museum of Modern Art collection, New York)

CALIGRAPH WITH 2 HEADS by Herbert Ferber

BRAZED BRONZE

(Courtesy of the André Emmerich Gallery)

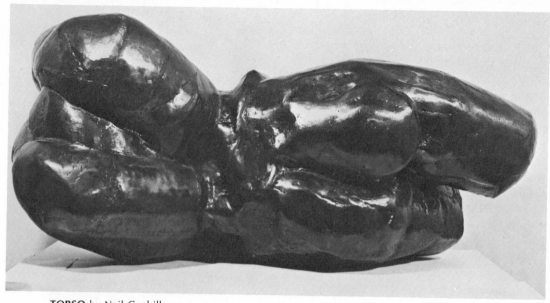

TORSO by Neil Cogbill

WELDED STEEL

(Photograph by the artist)

HOMAGE TO DAVID SMITH by Anthony Caro

WELDED STEEL PAINTED RED

(Courtesy of the André Emmerich Gallery)

NON-FERROUS METALS

One must know the peculiarities of non-ferrous metals before attempting to weld them. Non-ferrous metals are all the metals and alloys that do not contain iron. Copper, bronze, brass, aluminum, and the nickel alloys, *Monel* and *Inconel,* are the non-ferrous metals most frequently used in sculpture.

Copper

De-oxidized copper is the only kind of copper recommended for fusion welding. It contains a little silicon that dissolves the cupric oxides in the metal. Electrolytic copper contains oxygen that causes the metal to weaken when welded. It is possible to test the copper for this defect by heating it to a bright red and then hammering it on an anvil. If it flattens without breaking, it is probably de-oxidized and good enough for welding. Brazing rod and flux work very well on copper but if preserving the copper color is important, fusion welding with a de-oxidized copper welding rod is required.

Because copper expands and contracts more than most other metals, care must be taken to avoid distortions while welding. Some sculptors take advantage of this warpage and incorporate it into the form of the sculpture. Copper also conducts heat so rapidly that it usually requires a larger welding tip than that recommended for steel of the same thickness. If the piece being welded is quite large, it is better to back the area of the weld with asbestos sheets to reduce the loss of heat. A second torch handled by an assistant and directed in the area of the weld will help retain the heat necessary for welding. Like some of the other non-ferous metals,

SORCERER by Seymour Lipton

NICKEL-SILVER ON MONEL METAL

(Whitney Museum of American Art Collection, New York. Gift of the Friends of the Whitney Museum of American Art. Photograph by Oliver Baker)

copper melts suddenly and without warning. It may even collapse from the slightest .shock when the heat approaches the melting point.

Brass

Brass is an alloy of copper and zinc. It contains 10 to 40 percent zinc. When welding brass, it is important to avoid vaporizing the zinc as the fumes can cause nausea and dizziness. The loss of the zinc also weakens brass and causes a poor weld. This may be avoided by using a bronze welding rod with a low melting temperature, a good flux especially prepared for brazing and an oxidizing flame.

Bronze

Bronze is an alloy of copper and tin, and the same welding technique used for brass is recommended.

Aluminum

Aluminum is valued for its resistance to corrosion and its light weight. It is white in color and quite malleable in rolled forms. In cast forms it is very brittle. Aluminum does not change color as it reaches the welding temperature and, like copper, it will collapse very suddenly when near the melting point. Because aluminum conducts heat rapidly it is necessary to play the flame for a considerable time on the area to be welded. It should not be overheated,

however. If a soft stick rubbed on the hot metal leaves a black mark, the metal is hot enough to weld. The aluminum to be welded must be clean and free of oxide. A special flux for welding aluminum must be used and most of these give off irritating fumes. The flux is also corrosive to the metal. Therefore, the work should be washed after welding. A slightly carburizing flame makes the welding easier.

Monel and Inconel

Monel and Inconel are nickel alloys that resist corrosion and have a bright color and lustre. Sheets thinner than 16 gauge may be soldered, but fusion welding is recommended for thicker sheets. Bronze-welding flux is used with Monel but Inconel requires a special Inconel flux. Monel and Inconel welding rods are used.

WARRIORS by John Baldwin

WELDED COPPER

(James Mason Gunn Collection, Tallahassee, Florida)

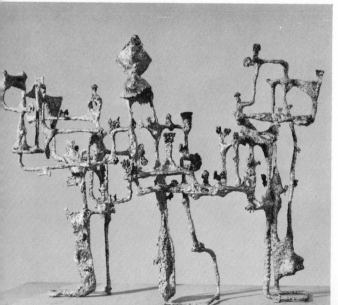

PROCESSION by Ibram Lassaw

WIRE, COPPER, VARIOUS BRONZES AND SILVER

(Whitney Museum of American Art Collection, New York. Photograph by Geoffrey Clements)

BRAZING

Brazing or bronze-welding is more like soldering than welding. The two pieces of metal are joined together with an alloy that does not mix with them autogenously. The parent metal must be heated above 1000°F but below its own melting point. At this temperature the bronze rod melts, coating the pieces to be joined or the surface to be covered. Brazing is useful for joining cast-iron and dissimilar metals but it is used by sculptors primarily for surfacing welded iron or steel sculptures. Bronze and nickel-silver are the two alloys most frequently used for this purpose.

Procedure

With a supply of bronze welding rods and flux handy, ignite the torch and adjust it to produce a slightly carburizing flame. Heat the area to be brazed with the tip of the flame held about ¼ to ½ inch from the surface. Heat the rod at the same time by holding it near the flame. When the rod is hot, dip it into the flux. It is not necessary to have a lot of flux on the rod. When the area being heated turns a dark red, place the tip of the rod on the spot to be brazed. The rod and the flux will melt, causing the molten bronze to spread over the pre-heated area. If two pieces are being joined, the bronze will flow along the join.

If the metal is too hot, the molten bronze will bubble and run. If it is too cold, it will form little balls and will not spread. When you have once formed a puddle of bronze and the metal has spread evenly, you can continue the process without interruption by moving the torch and rod along the join or into the adjacent areas. Be sure that the surfaces to be brazed are clean.

When the fluxed part of the rod is used up, dip it again into the flux. After brazing, the glass-like flux can be removed from the surface with a wire brush, small chisel or file.

MONARCH by John Baldwin

WELDED STEEL BRAZED WITH COPPER AND BRASS

(Mrs. George Birkenstein Collection, San Miguel Allende, Mex.,

FIGURE 6. Brazing

(Photograph by Doug Stewart)

FINISHING AND PRESERVING WELDED SCULPTURE

With the exception of the rare noble metals like gold and platinum, metals will deteriorate in time because of corrosive elements in the atmosphere. The fumes (smog) in all urban areas are very harmful. Even in pure air some degree of oxidation is continually occurring. Some metals are more resistant to corrosion than others, but the sculptor does not choose a metal only for its non-corrosive properties. Usually the ductility, malleability, strength, and rigidity are factors of greater concern to the creative sculptor. Therefore, some method of protecting the metal must be applied to the finished work.

In the past, efforts were made to preserve sculpture in whatever medium by applying waxes, oils, gums, and crude paints. These "finishes" were very temporary on sculpture exposed to the elements and it is likely that in early cultures periodic applications of protective coatings were in some way ritualistic. Today the synthetic resin coatings are so superior to the early paints, varnishes and gums that these have virtually disappeared from the market. One of the oldest and still effective synthetic coatings is Pyroxylin (Duco) made from nitrocellulose. There are many synthetic coatings available; cellulose acetate (acryloid), polymides (nylon), ureas mixed with oil—modified alkyds, polyesters and epoxys are but a few. However, when selecting a coating for a sculpture there are more points to con-

sider than permanence. We also look for something that is reasonably fast-drying, tough, reliable, colorless (clear coatings), colorfast (paints), water-proof and that has desired luster and excellent adherence.

Rust itself sometimes acts as a protective coating for indoor sculpture. After the first rapid discoloration, an arresting of the oxidation process occurs. Rust, while harmful if permitted to continue uncontrolled, is very beautiful and can give character and unity of color to a piece of welded steel sculpture. A controlled and accelerated method for achieving this is to coat the entire surface with a dilute solution of hydrochloric acid and water, about 1 to 50. A dilute solution of nitric acid may also be used. To stop the action of the acid on the metal, dip or coat the entire piece with an alkaline solution. Then wash it thoroughly with clean water and allow it to dry in the open air. If the rusted surface is coated with a clear finish, it will darken considerably.

Sculpture made with stainless steel presents no rust problem, provided that the heat from the welding has not destroyed the corrosion resistant properties.

Welded iron or steel is usually discolored and there may be quantities of carbon and slag on the surface. This can best be removed with a steel wire-brush, either by hand or attached to an electric power tool. Immediately coat the metal to protect it from the air.

Three ways to protect ferrous metal sculpture after it has been cleaned are: 1. Impart a corrosion-resistant non-ferrous metal to the surface by either electroplating, metal spraying or brazing with the oxy-acetylene torch. 2. Apply an opaque coating containing a pigment that completely hides and protects the metal. 3. Apply a clear coating that protects the metal but does not hide the surface.

Although the non-ferrous metals are more resistant to corrosion, some will tarnish if they are not given a protective coating of some kind. Traditionally, copper and bronze are patinated with chemicals to produce a rapid controlled discoloration. Aluminum and brass are usually left in their natural state, but brass will tarnish unless protected.

Patination of Metals

Here are some formulas for producing patinas on metal. Though there are many techniques for mixing and applying these formulas, the results cannot be guaranteed because of the many variants which include temperature, humidity, purity of ingredients, and the skill of the person applying them. The resulting colors of oxides or sulphides are very thin and should be protected with a coating of wax or one of the clear synthetics.

Bronze

APPLE GREEN

Sodium Chloride	10 oz.
Ammonium Chloride	10 oz.
Vinegar	½ gal.
Ammonia	½ pt.

Heat the bronze enough to make the solution sizzle when applied.

ANTIQUE GREEN

Copper Sulphate	6 oz.
Ammonium Chloride	1 oz.
Water	½ gal.

Rinse in water and dry.

BROWN SHADES

Potassium Sulphide	1 oz.
Barium Sulphide	2 oz.
Ammonia	¼ pt.
Water	2 gals.

Copper

ANTIQUE GREEN

Copper Nitrate	2 oz.
Vinegar	½ oz.
Water	1 pt.

Apply the warm solution to clean copper

Brass

BLUE

Sodium Thiosulphate	1 oz.
Lead Acetate	½ oz.
Water	½ pt.

Apply the warm solution to clean brass.

GREEN

Iron Sulphate	1 oz.
Copper Sulphate	1 oz.
Ammonium Carbonate	1 oz.
Water	½ gal.

ELECTRIC ARC WELDING

The electric arc is the best method for fusing and cutting extra thick metal. When working with heavy plate and structural steel, you may find the electric arc welding equipment indispensable. It is also useful for working with alloy steels and non-ferrous metals. The portable machines are practical studio equipment if heavy gauge metal is frequently welded.

The intense concentrated heat produced by electricity as it jumps through the air from one electrode to another is the principle behind arc welding. Its temperature is 6500° to 7000°F. Basically the equipment consists of a transformer that converts the high-voltage electricity from a generator or house line to usable low-voltage high-amperage current, usually up to only 40 volts but possibly as high as 300 amperes. The current is carried in a superflexible, large diameter cable (1) from the machine to an insulated electrode holder (2) that you hold in your hand. Another cable is clamped to the metal being welded or the metal welding table (3). An electrode (4), either metal, carbon or tungsten, is placed in the electrode holder and, with the current turned on, an arc is forced to jump between the electrode and the base metal. You hold this arc by skillfully maintaining the electrode at the proper distance and angle to the work. (Diagram 10.)

A metal electrode is used for simple welds in mild steel. The metal not only conducts the electric current creating the arc but also melts and fuses with the parent metal, forming part of the bead. For harder steels, flux-coated metal electrodes are used. A carbon electrode acts only as a conductor of electricity, allowing the arc to jump between itself and the base metal. When the heat from the arc forms a molten puddle, a filler rod is dipped into it as in oxy-acetylene welding. The carbon electrode is also used for cutting metal with the electric arc. The carbon must be very sharp and you should use 25 to 50 more amperes than you would for welding the same gauge metal.

Electric arc welding is not difficult, but like the oxy-acetylene technique, it

FIGURE 7. Arc Welding

(Photograph by Doug Stewart)

takes practice. The equipment is more specialized and you should therefore determine if the kind of welding you will be doing justifies the investment. It would be wiser to utilize the services of a welding shop that has the equipment for an occasional weld requiring the electric arc. However, if you are going to use the electric arc welder, it is very important that you wear the necessary protective clothing and take the proper safety precautions.

The voltage output is relatively low, so shocks from the equipment are more discomforting than serious. However, only an experienced electrician should work on the equipment if it breaks down. Never work on a damp or wet floor and always make sure you have adequate ventilation. The most important safety measure in using the electric arc equipment is to use protective clothing and eye shields. The arc produces harmful infrared and ultraviolet rays as well as a splatter of molten metals. Never watch an arc with the naked eye. Infrared light rays can damage your eyesight, and exposure to ultraviolet rays can cause intense pain in the eyes for as long as 18 hours. A helmet or face shield with a lens that removes almost 100 percent of the harmful rays, long sleeves, a leather apron, asbestos cloth leggings and gauntlet-type gloves are the items necessary for adequate protection. If the skin is not completely covered by some heavy material, severe "sunburn" may result after only one or two hours of welding.

Specialized Welding Techniques

In recent years the metals industry has developed many alloys with increased corrosion and wear resistance, and also low carbon alloy steels with up to 30 percent more strength than ordinary steel. These alloys require special welding techniques and equipment not usually available to the sculptor and, because of the high degree of specialization, not very suited to his usual

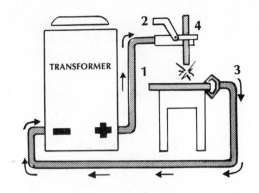

DIAGRAM 10. Electric-arc Welding Circuit

needs. Unless a sculptor is going to be welding alloys for a considerable length of time, it is not practical for him to either secure the expensive equipment or to learn the welding techniques required. It is better to take the work to a welding shop where such equipment is available, and have it done by trained operators.

Some of these specialized welding methods include such advanced techniques as fusion welding with ultra-high frequency vibrations and "cold" welding which utilizes high pressures to fuse the metal. Another industrial technique that has become useful to the sculptor is the combined metal-spray and welding process. The equipment takes about the same space as ordinary oxy-acetylene equipment and it can be a very practical tool in the studio. Another and more advanced metal spraying outfit feeds a metal wire into a melting chamber where propane and oxygen, both under pressure, produce a very hot flame that vaporizes the metal as it is ejected at supersonic speeds.

Other specialized welding techniques available are inert gas arc welding, especially useful in welding aluminum and some of the stainless steels, and atomic-hydrogen welding that produces a high temperature through the conversion of the gas from molecular hydrogen to atomic hydrogen and then back to molecular hydrogen again.

WELDED METAL "JUNK"

An abundant source of raw material for the direct-metal sculptors is found in the encroaching mountains of refuse that surround our major cities. Discarded tools, machines, automobiles, bedsteads, plumbing, etc. — all junk — provide a rich supply of stamped, forged and cast metal. Many of these items are also a source of exciting and meaningful imagery.

TIME MACHINE by Steve Waldeck

METAL ASSEMBLAGE

Early in our century the Dadaists and Surrealists made art out of common, everyday objects by dressing them up or by raising them, unchanged, to an exalted position. These "ready-mades" were at the time either shocking, provocative or amusing, depending upon the attitude of the viewer, and many of them have become historically and aesthetically significant. Hans Arp, one of the founders of Dada, in recounting its development has written, "We declared that everything that comes into being or is made by man is art." Marcel Duchamp exploited the magical transformations that occurred when ordinary objects were placed on pedestals or slightly altered. Since sculpture was made to satisfy the bourgeoisie tastes prevalent at that time, these "found objects" stimulated a response in the beholder not usually evoked. It was up to the viewer to make his own metaphorical associations, imagine the missing parts and act as agent in the metamorphosis that took place.

The alterations Duchamp made on some of these familiar objects were startling, to say the least. The famous mustache he painted on the reproduction of the Mona Lisa aroused all the indignation he had hoped for. Ordinary objects that he chose to exalt were presented as they had always been, but in a new environment they were seen in a new light — perhaps *seen* for the first time. His *choosing* of a particular object was considered the creative act. Herbert Read, in his *Concise History of Modern Sculpture*, says:

> The objects chosen by Duchamp — a wheel, a bottlerack, a urinal (upside down), a snow shovel, a comb, a hat-rack suspended from the ceiling, etc., may conceivably have some unconscious association for the artist; and if not the object itself, its configuration or Gestalt may have some hidden significance.

Some junk objects are selected solely

for their aesthetic or decorative qualities. The significant form inherent in a piece of machinery or a part of it, may delight the artist to the extent that he is moved to isolate it for his own satisfaction and to exhibit it so that others may enjoy it as well. When the formal or sculptural considerations are dominant in the selection or fabrication of "junk," it can be more legitimately classified as sculpture. John Chamberlain's agglomerates of dented and crushed automobile bodies excite the senses directly through their form and color without arousing our indignation over mass slaughter on the highways. On the other hand, the associative, connotative or literal aspects may dominate if, for example, the "ready-made" consists of a dirty hypodermic syringe resting on a bloody wad of cotton next to a scorched bottle cap. This assemblage of "ordinary things" makes a shocking social comment, but it is hardly *sculpture*. These presentations of three-dimensional objects defy the traditional concepts of sculpture, so they are loosely referred to as "Objects," "Tableaux," "Assemblages," or just simply "3-D."

When a sculptor assembles his creations from scrapped machine parts, setting them in motion is an obvious development. Incongruous arrangements of gears, belts, pulleys, wheels, cams, plungers, and rods all spinning, jerking and oscillating without apparent purpose are noisy, satirical protests against an age of over-mechanization. Such kinetic sculpture may cause one to ask if anything makes sense in today's mad, mad world. One of Jean Tinguely's machines was designed to destroy itself in a delightful frenzy. That suggests one answer.

Not all kinetic sculpture comes under the category of "junk." Alexander Calder's famous mobiles, the forerunners of modern kinetic art, and George Rickey's delicately balanced, precision-made "wind machines" adhere more

Steel Sculpture by Mario Cravo

WELDED INDUSTRIAL SCRAP

(Courtesy of the Institute of Contemporary Arts, Washington, D.C.)

JOHNNY BIRD by John Chamberlain

WELDED STEEL AUTOMOBILE SCRAP

(Courtesy of Martha Jackson Gallery. Photograph by Rudolph Burckhardt)

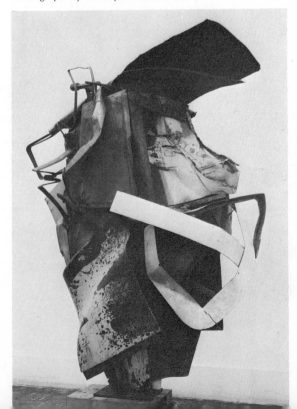

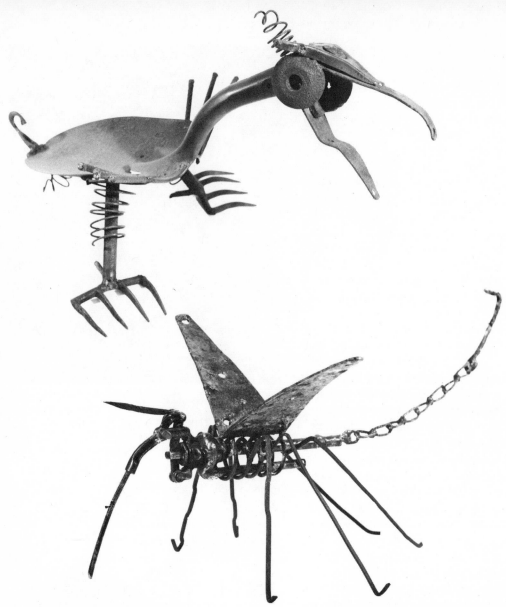

Shown on these two pages are student exercises made from junk. The two on the left were made from the junk shown in Figures 8 and 9.

(Photographs by the author)

FIGURE 8.

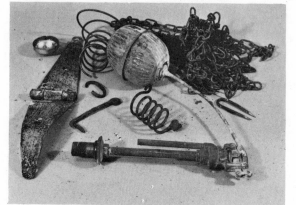

to the classic concepts of form and beauty.

It is possible to use scrap metal for welded sculpture and change its character to such a degree that no vestige of its original form or use is left. Naturally, when the found-object serves only as raw material for the creation of a new form, the resulting sculpture is not considered "junk." Mario Cravo's work is an example of this.

The "making" of junk sculpture may be undertaken as a very serious act of creation, or it can be approached lightly, with tongue in cheek. Whatever the intent, the amount and kind of welding involved will depend upon the nature of the objects, how much they will be altered, and how many will be assembled to create the desired image. In some instances only the cutting torch is needed to eliminate extraneous and distracting elements. It is possible that a found-object will only need welding to a base, while the assembling of a complex form may require cutting, welding and brazing.

FIGURE 9.

FIGURE 10. Welding goggles and leather gloves after many hours of use. The lenses are spotted by the tiny particles of hot metal that fly up from the work. The left-hand glove shows the effects of handling sharp-edged, hot metals.

(*Photograph by the author*)

SAFETY TIPS

1. Clear the welding area of all combustibles for a distance of thirty feet. If this cannot be done, erect a flame-proof screen.

2. Be sure the equipment is properly set up and in good working condition.

3. Never use oil or grease on welding equipment.

4. The cylinders should be chained to a wall or a welding cart in an upright position. Never drop or roll them.

5. Check for leaks periodically around all connections and along the hose. Use grease-free soapy water.

6. Don't stand in front of cylinder valves when opening them.

7. Don't open the acetylene valve more than one turn. Leave the wrench in place for an emergency shut-down.

8. Wear protective clothing—no cuffs or loose folds. High laced shoes prevent sparks from burning your feet.

9. Always wear welding goggles when welding or cutting.

10. When the cylinders are empty close the valves and replace the valve cap. Mark an "E" for empty.

11. Never force the connections or the valves.

12. Always have a good fire extinguisher, sand or water handy.

13. Never flame-cut into containers or drums without knowing what they formerly contained. Residue of combustible fluids could cause an explosion.

HEAD by Julio Gonzalez, 1935?
WROUGHT IRON
The Museum of Modern Art Collection, New York

IN MEMORIAM by John Baldwin

FIBERGLASS

(Photograph by Doug Stewart)

PART III

FIBERGLASS REINFORCED PLASTICS:

A New Medium for Sculpture

Credit for the vitality of sculpture in the first half of the twentieth century cannot be attributed to any single person, movement or technical discovery. The influences were to heterogeneous and the results have been too diverse for any simple cause and effect relationships. I have already mentioned the importance of metal welding techniques for twentieth century artists who had been liberated by new theories and philosophies of art and were impatient to create new forms. The metals these artists shaped were, for the most part, not new. With the exception of some of the new alloys, the welded metals are those that have been used since antiquity. It was the new tools — the welding techniques — that made possible a direct, fluid handling of metal which no sculptor had known before.

Another revolutionary development in sculpture which can only accelerate its already dynamic proliferations and open up a whole new world of three-dimensional form is the use of glass reinforced plastics. Glass fibers coated with polymerized organic resins offer the artist more than a new tool; they offer a new medium, a material waiting to be shaped, formed, molded, cast and fabricated into anything his imagination can conjure.

Plastics

Since celluloid was discovered in 1868 by John Hyatt in response to a $10,000 prize offered to anyone who could find a substitute for ivory, the plastics industry has progressed at a fantastic rate. At the turn of the century, celluloid billiard balls, shirt collars, combs and plastic Victorian bric-a-brac were a sign of industrial progress. However, it was not until the development of *Bakelite,* named after its discoverer, Leo Bakeland, in 1909, that the full industrial potential of plastics was realized. Soon many different kinds of plastics were developed, each with its own specific advantages and disadvantages. During World War II there was a great need to find substitutes for natural materials such as rubber that were no longer available to us. The aircraft industry needed materials that could be easily formed or molded into strong, light sections that would stand the stresses of high speed flight. And due to military priorities, plastic substitutes took

1

1. MASQUERADE (detail) by John Baldwin

FIBERGLASS

(Photograph by Doug Stewart)

2. STABAT MATER by John Baldwin

FIBERGLASS

(Photograph by Doug Stewart)

3. ALCHEMY by John Baldwin

FIBERGLASS, POLYESTER RESIN AND METALLIC POWDERS

(Photograph by Doug Stewart)

3

2

the place of common, everyday metal articles in the home. Today, plastics play an important role in everything from orbiting satellites and world-girdling strato-jets to sewer lines and subterranean moisture barriers.

Definition

Any material that can be shaped, formed or molded is considered plastic. A material that can be continually flexed in any direction without breaking apart is also plastic. Today there are many loose and ambiguous usages of the word. To avoid adding to the confusion, I prefer to borrow a definition from the introduction to Reginald L. Wakeman's book, *The Chemistry of Commercial Plastics:*

plastics . . . as its use has developed in American industry, it now covers a large group of organic substances, either wholly or in part synthetic, which can be molded into coherent solid articles that retain their shape indefinitely at room temperature. In the stricter sense . . . it refers specifically to molded articles which, themselves, are not plastic in the usual dictionary sense, but which are formed from materials that are plastic and hence moldable at some stage during the process of fabrication.

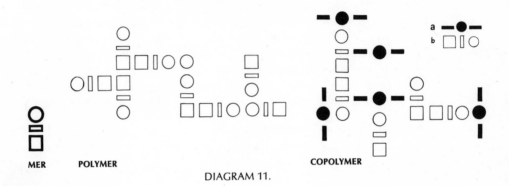

MER   POLYMER   COPOLYMER

DIAGRAM 11.

POLYMERS

Nearly all of the plastics are made from organic substances consisting of exceptionally large molecules. These molecules are made up of units called mers. A monomer is a single combination of linked elements that is ready to join other monomers. Two such units of linked elements form a dimer. Many monomers combined in a chain-like pattern result in a polymer. If different monomers are linked in a pattern, a copolymer is formed. Five hundred or more repeating units are known as "high" polymers. It is the "high" polymers that make up most of the synthetic resin molecules. (Diagram 11.)

Synthetic Resins

The raw materials from which the plastics are formed are derived from coal, petroleum, natural gas, air, water, sand, salt, lime, cellulose and sulphur. From these the chemists extract carbon, oxygen, hydrogen, chlorine, fluorine, and nitrogen which are used in various combinations to make the resinous substances that are the base of all plastics. The building up of compounds by the union of their basic elements or by the union of other simpler compounds is by definition a synthesis. Thus the plastics are often referred to as synthetics.

There are over twenty basic plastics in use at the present time, known by well over a thousand trade names. The basic plastics may be combined to form new plastics, and these totally new or improved combinations are appearing on the market under new trade names that are nearly impossible to pronounce and help little in identifying the basic materials from which they are made. The artist, if he is to use plastics and take advantage of their desirable characteristics without being discouraged by their limitations, should acquire at least a general understanding of the nature of these complex materials.

Most of the plastics used by industry are not suited to the artist's needs because to mold them requires high temperatures and high pressures that can be achieved only under controlled factory conditions. Molds designed to provide these high pressures and controlled high temperatures are capable of mass producing only relatively small and simple forms such as pot handles, small radio housings, tooth brushes, tableware, and the like. The larger and more complex forms are produced with low or room temperature resins requiring little or no pressure. These are the resins most suitable for studio use.

Thermoplastic and Thermosetting

Plastics are grouped into two categories for the sake of simplicity and convenience: thermoplastic and thermosetting. The thermoplastics are made up of a tangled maze of long, chain-like molecules that become active when heated and because of their tendency to slip and slide, the material becomes flexible and capable of being formed. When the plastic is cooled again, the molecules lie quiet and the plastic retains its new form at room temperature. If reheated, the plastic again becomes flexible and the forming process may be repeated. (Diagram 12.) The thermosetting plastics consist of chain-like molecules similar to those in thermoplastics. However, these chains are capable of cross-linking when subjected to heat, high pressure or catalysis, thus forming a three-dimensional structure that holds the molecules firmly together. Once polymerization has taken place, these cross-linked molecular structures are permanently fixed and will not return to flexible or fluid state under heat or pressure. (Diagram 13.) Following is a list of thermosetting and thermoplastic resins useful to the sculptor:

Thermoplastic

RESIN	COMMERCIAL FORM	STUDIO USE
Acrylics (Methyl and Methacrylate)	Clear, transluscent and opaque solids, liquid resins, molding powder	Fabricating, casting, coating
Cellulosics	Molding powder, liquid, solids	Casting, coating, mold release agent
Fluorocarbons	Molding powder, granules, liquid resin	Release agent, molds

RESIN	COMMERCIAL FORM	STUDIO USE
Polyethylene	Powder, pellets, sheet, rod, tube, foamed	Molding, casting, coating
Polypropylene	Molding compounds, film, fiber, sheeting	Molding, casting, coating
Polystyrene	Molding powder, granules, sheets, rods, foamed block, liquid resin	Molding, foam casting, fabricating, coating
Vinyls	Powder, liquid resin, film, sheets	Coating, release agent, casting, molding

Thermosetting

RESIN	COMMERCIAL FORM	STUDIO USE
Amino resins (Urea and Melamine)	Molding powder, granules, liquid resin	Adhesives, castings, laminates
Epoxy	Molding compounds, liquid resins, foamed blocks	Strong adhesives, laminates, castings, coatings, etc. (unlimited)
Phenolics	Molding powder, solids, granules, liquid resins	Adhesives, laminates, coatings, castings
Poyester resins (unsaturated)	Liquid resins, molding compounds, solid sheets, rods, tubes	Laminating, coatings, casting, fabricating
Silicones	Liquid resins, greases, synthetic rubber	Mold release agent, flexible molds, mixed with other resins for coatings

DIAGRAM 12. Thermoplastic

1. Chain of resting thermoplastic molecules at room temperature. The plastic is stiff and holds its shape.

2. If heated, the molecules become active. The plastic is soft and malleable.

3. Cooled to room temperature, the plastic holds its new shape. The process of heating, forming and cooling may be repeated innumerable times.

DIAGRAM 13. Thermosetting

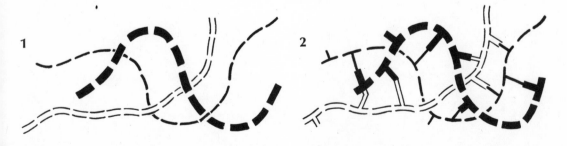

1. Chainlike molecules are capable of cross-linking if acted upon by heat, pressure or a catalyst.

2. Cross-linked molecules form a premanent, three-dimensional structure that will not return to a soft or fluid state if re-exposed to heat or pressure.

TERMINOLOGY

In this age of specialization the creative artists cannot be expected to have the same technical knowledge of synthetic plastics as a highly specialized chemist. It is sufficient for the artist to know the working properties of each material, and this is usually learned by trial and error. Industrial techniques are helpful only up to a point because mass production methods based on a unit-cost philosophy are not related to the artist's creation of a unique object. He is not deeply concerned with its marketability. He is probably more interested in the result of improvisation than plan. However, some knowledge of plastics is essential to better anticipate the possibilities and limitations of the medium, to be prepared to take full advantage of the "happy accidents" that may occur, and at the very least, to become aware of the wide variety of plastic materials available.

The following list of terms used frequently in any discussion of plastics is intended to help clarify some of the technical jargon:

Accelerators, promoters—Chemical additives that speed the polymerization of molecules.

Anti-oxidant—A substance that reduces the undesirable effects of oxidation on a material exposed to the air.

Binder—A liquid that holds pigments or other particles together and, upon drying, cements them to each other and to the underlying surface.

Catalyst, hardener—Those chemicals that induce a chemical reaction but are not affected by it themselves. Usually the catalyst is separated and removed once it has done its work, but in plastics it can become part of the polymerized resin.

Cure, set—The new physical state of a substance after it has been chemically changed through heat or catalytic action.

Emulsion—The suspension of a very fine oily or resinous liquid in another liquid.

Exotherm—Having to do with the amount and the rate of heat given off by a chemical reaction.

Foamed plastics, expanded or cellular plastics—A spongy, solid plastic that is up to thirty times greater in volume than the parent liquid components from which it was made. There is no increase in weight.

Gel—Jelly-like state of a colloidal solution in its solid phase. That state achieved by a resin before cure.

Gel coat—A thin layer of resin, usually thixotropic, and containing pigments or coloring agents either applied as a first coat in a mold or as a last coat on hand-built work.

Inhibitors, retarders—Chemicals that slow down a chemical reaction.

Laminate—Several layers of plastic coated fillers or reinforcing material combined by heat and/or pressure to form a single sheet.

Lay-up—Arranging and saturating reinforcing materials in a mold or over a form.

Mold release, parting agent, separator—A surface coating to prevent the sticking of one substance to another. To prevent molded or cast forms from sticking to the mold.

Plasticity—The ability to be shaped and formed by plastic flow.

Plasticizer—A chemical agent added to plastic compositions to make them softer and more flexible.

Polymerization—The combining together of two or more molecules into a larger single molecule.

Pot life—The working time one has after the catalyst or hardener has been added to the resin and before it gels in the pot.

Resin—A non-crystallizing solid or semi-solid organic substance obtained in nature or made synthetically, consisting of unusually large molecules.

Shelf life—The length of time a plastic will remain usable in storage. Heat, contamination and time will eventually result in spontaneous catalyzation and cure.

Solvent—A substance, usually liquid, that loosens or dissolves other substances.

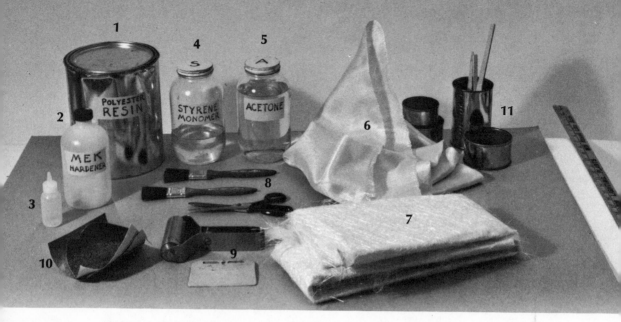

FIGURE 10. Basic equipment and supplies for making fiberglass reinforced plastic sculpture. **1.** Polyester resin. **2.** MEK peroxide (hardener). **3.** Squeeze bottle. **4.** Styrene monomer. **5.** Acetone. **6.** Fiberglass cloth. **7.** Fiberglass mat. **8.** Pure bristle brushes and scissors. **9.** Roller and squeegee. **10.** Sandpaper. **11.** Tin cans and stirring sticks.

FIGURE 11. Auxiliary equipment and supplies. **1.** Additives (Sanding Aid and Thixogel). **2.** Melamine-coated fiberglass mat. **3.** Chopped fiberglass strands. **4.** Fiberglass tape. **5.** Metallic powders (bronze, aluminum, copper). **6.** Coloring agents. **7.** Fillers (sawdust, calcium silicate, asbestos shorts). **8.** Nylon yarn. **9.** Heat lamp. **10.** Measuring beaker. **11.** Metal shears. **12.** Spatulas, modeling tools and wood rasp. **13.** Mold release.

(Photographs by the author)

FIBERGLASS REINFORCED PLASTIC SCULPTURE

Fiberglass reinforced plastics, or F.R.P. as it is called in industry, appears to be the most versatile plastic medium suited to the needs of the sculptor. The fact that polyester and epoxy resins will polymerize at room temperature without applied pressure makes it possible for large, complex glass-reinforced forms to be hand built in the studio. The many positive features of this medium so outweigh the few negative characteristics that it comes close to being the ideal sculpture material. When polyester or epoxy resins saturate woven fiberglass cloth, the resulting cured fabric rivals any other material in a strength-to-weight ratio, and the forming possibilities are limitless. With imagination and a little ingenuity, any three-dimensional form may be realized.

Perhaps the main advantage in using fiberglass reinforced resins lies in what might at first seem to be a great disadvantage—the medium's lack of character in its raw, formative state. Wood and stone with their inherent beauty of grain and color are capable of exciting the senses and even directing the "thinking" hand. But filled or reinforced plastic before gelation is a colorless, gooey, sticky mess. An uncured, fiberglass-filled resin lacks even the tactility of moist clay or wet plaster. All other media have enough inherent character — plasticity, hardness, grain, color, etc., to impose a degree of formal autonomy . . . "truth to materials."

Because of the inherent lack of character, the fiberglass reinforced plastics might be considered as the least specialized of all the sculpture media and, therefore, the most adaptable. In a formal sense, it is the most "plastic" since it can be utilized as either an additive or subtractive medium and it may be used either directly — for modeling and hand lay-up work—or indirectly—as casting and molding material.

Formal Characteristics

The fiberglass reinforced plastics medium lends itself more naturally to forms having broad expanses of surface because fiberglass is at its optimum strength as a woven or mat fabric. Laminations of the fiberglass fabric saturated with polyester or epoxy resin are easily formed and stretched into complex, twisting, convoluted, planar surfaces slicing through space, or as an outer skin enclosing a great deal of volume. These shell-like structures, because of their multi-directional surfaces, multiply many times the normal weight-mass-strength ratios. Also, the fluid consistency of the resin before gelation makes brushing, flowing, spraying or rolling practical techniques for spreading the resin over broad surfaces.

This does not mean that it is wrong to use fiberglass reinforced resins in some other way. It is possible to make casts using resins filled with chopped fiberglass strands. Modeling compounds made of fiberglass filled resins and other fillers are being successfully used. Preformed fiberglass laminates are capable of being cut and assembled into translucent constructions with exciting spacial dimensions. And resin-saturated chopped fiberglass strands sprayed over complex forms may impart a hard, strong surface to an otherwise fragile substance. These are only a few of the possible methods of utilizing the fiberglass reinforced resins, but none is as structurally efficient as the broad laminated surfaces made of plastic-saturated fibrous glass.

A Place to Work

Do not use polyester resin in your home unless you work close to an exhaust vent. The pungent odor that drifts into every corner does not respect closed doors and will even penetrate every floor of a five story building. The odor persists long after the lids are back on the jars and cans. A studio away from the house is preferable, and it should be equipped to maintain a steady working temperature close to 70°F while at the same time affording maximum ventilation. This is not easy to achieve. The doors and windows must be closed to maintain the 70°F in winter. In summer an air-conditioner works very well for controlling the temperature and humidity but, again, the doors and windows must remain shut.

While working on a large commission one summer, I had to install air-conditioning to control the excessive humidity that was inhibiting the polymerization of the resin. The air-conditioner cut down the humidity efficiently but the studio became so chilled that the polymerization was again retarded. Finally I had to resort to heat lamps in order to speed up the setting and curing of the resin. By this time the air in the room affected me like tear gas. The doors and windows could not be opened while the air-conditioner was on.

The work area should have good light, running water and drainage, and the source of heat should be a safe distance away from the work and storage area. A smooth and hard floor will facilitate cleaning and minimize the tipping of cans, jars and bottles. A shop vacuum is very useful for cleaning up all of the glass fibers and dust that accumulate in a day's work.

Spread newspapers where you are mixing and working and dispose of them at frequent intervals to reduce odor and fire hazard.

MIXING AND LAMINATING

Get everything ready before beginning an experimental lamination of fiberglass and polyester resin. Plenty of clean cans or paper cups, mixing sticks, paper towels and newspapers should be handy. The resin, catalyst (MEK) and solvents or cleaners should also be open and ready. Place brushes and whatever other tools you plan to use as well as any fillers and additives within reach. The fiberglass mat and cloth should be cut to the necessary shape and size.

Since it takes thirty to forty minutes for a catalyzed polyester resin to set, you must plan how much glass you can saturate in that time and catalyze only that much resin. The thickness of the cloth and mat, the complexity of the forms and the accessibility of the work will determine how much you can accomplish. The room temperature and the amount of catalyst added to the resin will alter the working time or pot life. Except in the case of broad, flat expanses such as boat hulls, tanks, skylights, and sinks, not much fibrous glass can be saturated in thirty minutes. I usually mix only about ¼ beer can or three ounces of resin at a time. For the kind of work I usually do, this quantity takes about thirty minutes to apply.

The amount of catalyst to be added to an ounce of resin varies with the room temperature, the resin temperature (usually a room heats up faster than the liquids in it), the consistency and condition of the resin, the amount being mixed, and the ultimate thickness of the application. Thick coats or laminations set up faster than thin coats and need less catalyst. If too much catalyst is used there will be too much exotherm (generated heat) and it might result in cracking and warping. If too little catalyst is added, the resin may never cure, and remain sticky forever! Under normal conditions at 70°F most polyesters call for about ten drops of MEK peroxide (catalyst) to the ounce. With practice this can be judged pretty accurately without actually counting up to 20, 30 and 40 drops. I usually pour an amount of resin in the can and then *squirt* the squeeze bottle of catalyst into it several times. I judge the number of squirts needed by the way the previous batch set up. Sometimes I goof. If you misjudge often, go back to counting.

You will be able to judge just how much resin is needed to saturate a given amount of glass, mat or cloth only through practice. For this reason it is a good idea to have more than one sculpture going at a time. Any catalyzed resin that may be left in the mixing can may be applied to the second sculpture. I usually keep as many as five going at one time and program my work in the studio so as to minimize waste.

It may help to know that it takes about two ounces to saturate one square foot of 7½-ounce fiberglass cloth. This is taken from boat covering charts. Sculpture forms are not usually so simple.

The thickness of the laminate necessary to provide strength to a given form depends on the area to be spanned, the weight it must support and how well the overall form is *engineered*. A thin laminate that is properly designed will support more weight and withstand more stress than a thick one that is not. Fiberglass laminates in industry range in thickness from $\frac{1}{16}$ inch to ½ inch. I make it a rule, regardless of size, to have a minimum of three layers of glass in every part of the sculpture — alternate layers of mat-cloth-mat or cloth-mat-cloth, depending on the temporary supports and the complexity of the form.

Following is a series of photographs that illustrate the procedure for making a fiberglass-reinforced polyester laminate.

Mixing and Laminating

1. Pour about three ounces of polyester resin into a clean can.

2. Add twenty or thirty drops or about three good squirts of catalyst (MEK).

3. Mix thoroughly into the resin.

4. Brush on the thoroughly mixed catalyzed resin and work it into the fiberglass cloth.

5. When the cloth is completely saturated carefully place a piece of fiberglass mat over it.

6. Work more of the resin into the mat by pressing and pouncing the brush. If fiberglass mat is brushed, the fibers will pull and bunch up into lumps.

7. When the mat is saturated, place another piece of fiberglass cloth on top of it and continue saturating it with resin.

8. Work out all air bubbles with the brush; on flat work with a hard backing, a roller or squeegee may be used.

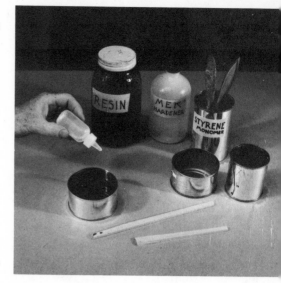

2

5

6

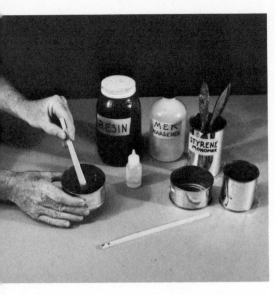

3

4

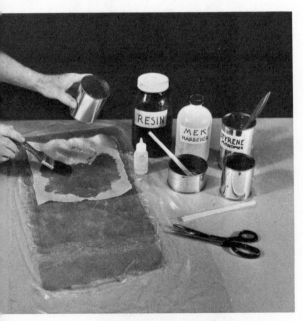

7

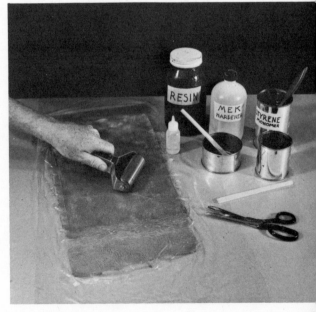

8

1. **HIROSHIMA '45** by John Baldwin
   FIBERGLASS
   (Photograph by Doug Stewart)

2. **Untitled Sculpture** by Mordi Gerstein
   FIBERGLASS AND EPOXY RESIN OVER BALLOONS
   (Photograph by the artist)

3. **Untitled Sculpture** by Pat Kelly
   MOLDED FIBERGLASS PAINTED WITH LACQUER
   (Photograph by Doug Stewart)

4. **TROPHY** by John Baldwin
   FIBERGLASS, POLYESTER RESIN, BRONZE POWDER
   (Photograph by Doug Stewart)

AGGRESSOR by John Baldwin
FIBERGLASS
(Photograph by Doug Stewart)

STATISTIC by John Baldwin
FIBERGLASS
(Photograph by Doug Stewart)

1

2

3

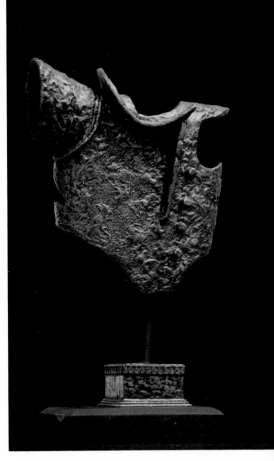

4

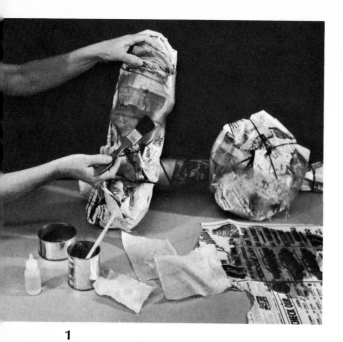
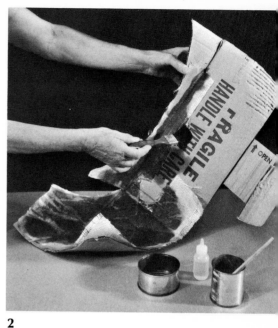

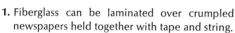

1.   2.

1. Fiberglass can be laminated over crumpled newspapers held together with tape and string.

2. Cardboard structures, pinned and glued together, make excellent supports for fiberglass laminates. The cardboard usually becomes part of the laminate.

3. Papier mâché makes an excellent *core* for fiberglass sculpture, providing it is absolutely dry before laminating.

4. Chicken wire and hardware cloth are easily formed into temporary supports. The fiberglass

cloth can be held in place by looping short lengths of wire through it or by clipping it in place with spring operated clothespins. The wire will separate from the cloth as soon as the laminate is rigid.

5. Fiberglass cloth, suspended and pulled into shape with strings to achieve a free drape effect, can be easily saturated with resin by backing it with a small piece of cardboard as the brushing proceeds.

6. Fiberglass cloth or tape may be draped over and around metal and wood armatures. It may be presaturated or the resin may be brushed on in place.

ARMATURES

VARIOUS TEMPORARY SUPPORTS FOR STARTING FIBERGLASS SCULPTURE

The form that you wish to create in fiberglass reinforced plastics will have to be supported temporarily until the resin sets. There is no limit to the kinds of supports you may use, providing they are dry. Water inhibits the polymerization of catalyzed polyester resin. These armatures need only hold the limp, saturated fiberglass until the resin sets and the laminate can support itself. The support can be left permanently inside

the sculpture or it can be removed before the entire surface is covered and the form becomes closed. In the case of sculpture having openings where the interior forms are as aesthetically important as the exterior forms, such as the "Stabat Mater" (color plate page 72), the entire internal, temporary support is removed and the interior surfaces are textured and finished with the same attention given to the exterior surfaces.

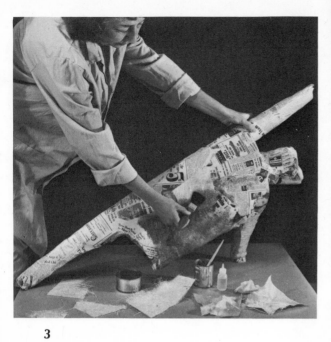

3

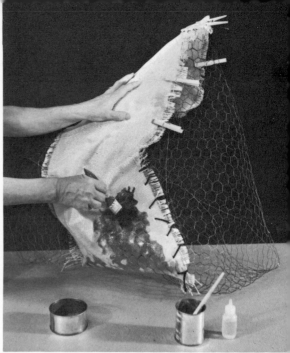

4

6

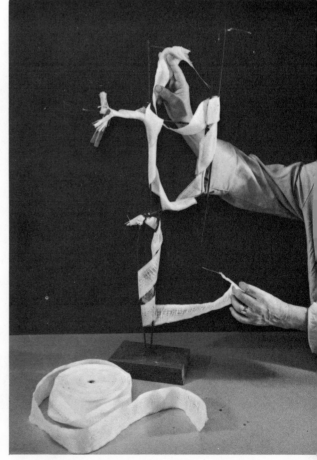

5

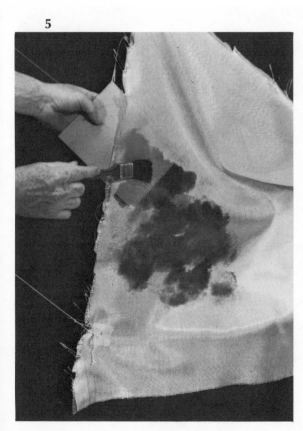

JOB by John Baldwin

FIBERGLASS

(Dee Preusch and Martha L. Ware Collection, Washington, D. C.)

PHALANX by John Baldwin

FIBERGLASS

(Mr. and Mrs. Gerard Baldwin Collection, Los Angeles. Photograph by Doug Stewart)

Girl with Book by Giorgio I. Spadaro

FIBERGLASS, POLYESTER RESIN, ASBESTOS FIBERS, PIGMENTS AND SAND. The form was modeled over a water soluble core. When finished, the core was removed with hot water.

(Photograph by the artist)

FIGURE by Mordi Gerstein

FIBERGLASS AND EPOXY RESIN OVER BALLOONS

(Photograph by the artist)

TRIUMPHANT by John Baldwin

FIBERGLASS

(Lester Henderson Collection, Danville, California. Photograph by the author)

1

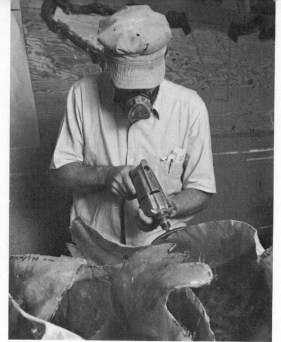

2

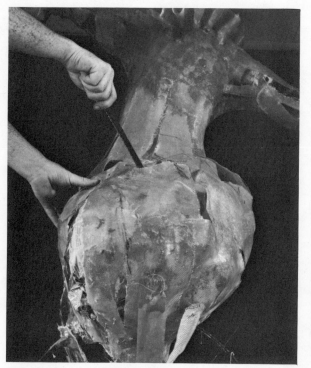

3

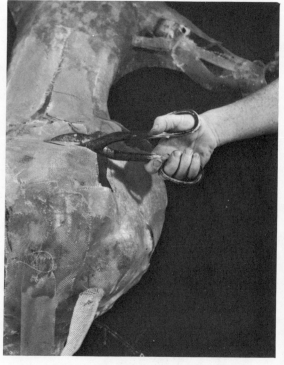

4

Building Up and Cutting Down

As the sculpture develops from armature or temporary support toward its final form, certain changes must be made. Additional laminations may be applied directly over the already hard, cured fiberglass forms. Some sanding on the old work is necessary before the new work is laid down. The sanding removes the minute, stiff fibers of glass that stick up from the surface, preventing the new work from completely contacting the old (2). Some device must be employed to keep the fiberglass from sliding off vertical or steeply inclined surfaces. Clipping the work with spring-type clothespins, tying it with string or thin wires looped through previously drilled holes, or pushing round toothpicks through the fiberglass into 1/32-inch drilled holes are methods that have worked (1). For the sculptor, ingenuity is as important as talent. When cutting and trimming, the thickness of the laminate determines which tools and what methods should be used. Thin sections can be cut easily with large metal shears as shown in **4**. A hack-saw blade is recommended for thicker sections (3). The best time to cut into or trim fiberglass laminates of any thickness is right after the resin gels. It is dry to the touch but rubbery. With a mat knife or any sharp blade you can cut the gelatinous material as easily as cheese (1).

(Photographs by the author)

Work in Progress

The photograph above shows my studio with a few fiberglass sculptures in various stages of development. I generally work on a number of pieces simultantously. This proves economical in both time and material. While the resin is setting on one, I can work on another, and any resin left in the mixing can is used up on one of the other pieces. Usually I employ several different kinds of temporary supports in each piece.

At far left, **JOB** was built on a support of cardboard, paper and wood. All of it was removed. In the center, **HIROSHIMA '45** was formed with burlap draped over a welded steel armature. The rough texture of the burlap was preserved. Hanging to the right of center, **SAMOTHRACIAN** is shown just after the fiberglass cloth and tape, which had been supported by a system of strings stretched from all parts of the studio, had become set and self supporting. The form was further strengthened with more laminations of fiberglass cloth, mat and putty.

The photograph at left shows **SENTRY** in its initial state. The rough burlap has just been draped over a support of thin sticks from old window shades. Some string was used to pull the burlap taut. When the desired gesture was established, the burlap itself was saturated with catalyzed polyester resin to stiffen it. Then the form was laminated only on the inside with fiberglass cloth and mat in order to preserve the coarse burlap texture on the exterior surfaces. When the draped form was strong and rigid, some of the sticks were replaced with welded steel rods. The legs, spear and cincture were covered with fiberglass tape and putty.

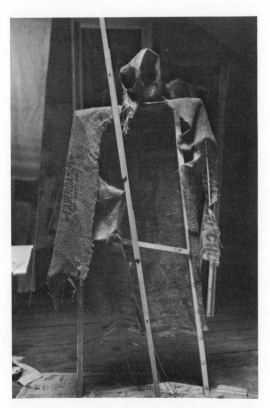

THE POLYESTERS

The resins most widely used for reinforced plastics are the unsaturated polyesters. In fact, it has been estimated that these resins account for about 90 percent of the total reinforced plastics output. With so many good resins available, this widespread adoption by industrial users as well as sculptors is due to the following advantages: 1. Easy application of the liquid resin. 2. The resin cures rapidly at room temperature and without giving off volatile by-products. 3. Its dimensional stability is excellent. 4. Large complex forms are possible without the use of costly pressure molds. 5. Its general physical characteristics are good. 6. A variety of finishes is possible through the use of additives, modifiers and fillers.

The polyesters also have a wider range of properties than any of the other polymers. Many molding and casting techniques are possible, ranging from the production of one-piece boat hulls 80 feet long, layed up by hand in an open contact mold, to tiny electronic components cast in multiple encapsulation molds.

There are at least a dozen industrial molding techniques for which polyesters are suited. The sculptor cannot take advantage of all of these as the necessary equipment is highly specialized and is only economically feasible if a large quantity of identical articles is to be produced.

Many varieties of coatings have been developed from the polyester resins. These coatings have excellent weathering and sealing properties and are also highly resistant to chemicals, abrasion and heat. They are used on metal, wood, cement, and other less durable materials. Defensite LG is one such polyester coating.

When the basic polyester resin is dissolved in a special monomer such as styrene, and catalyzed, a cross-linkage takes place in the linear molecular chains, resulting in a copolymer thermoset of polyester and monomer. The monomer serves both as solvent and vehicle for the extremely viscous polyester molecules. Styrene is the monomer most used in this polymerization because of its relatively low cost, its compatibility and reactivity with polyesters, its high strength properties, and the absence of volatile by-products in curing.

The percentage of styrene to unsaturated polyester is critical since it affects the strength and resistance to chemicals of the cured resins. An excess of styrene will adversely affect the curing process itself. Because this balance of polyester and styrene is established in the liquid resins by the manufacturer, it is not advisable to thin them further by adding more styrene. If it becomes necessary to lower the viscosity for easier saturation of the reinforcement material, use the very minimum necessary to accomplish this end.

The catalysts used for setting-up the polyester resins are not true catalysts because they are not removed from the curing resin after the cross-linking has been triggered. It is an addition reaction that takes place and no volatile by-products are released. The "catalyst" activates those parts of the molecular chains capable of cross-linking and, having done this, is incorporated into the resulting copolymer. Organic peroxides are the principal "catalysts" used.

The unsaturated polyester resins usually contain an inhibitor that retards spontaneous polymerization, thus prolonging the shelf-life, or storage life, of the resin. This inhibitor also prolongs the working time (pot life or gel time) of the resin before gelation takes place. Once gelation does take place, the resin can no longer be worked. The "catalyst" breaks down and counteracts the inhibitor. There is also an activator (cobalt) present in the resin which acts upon the "catalyst" when it is added. It decomposes the "catalyst," releasing active free radicals that spark the cross-linking process without the use of heat. (Diagram 14.)

When purchasing polyester resins it is important to know the working characteristics, and this information is available from the manufacturer. In addition to the viscosity and curing characteristics of the resin, you should also know the physical, mechanical and weathering characteristics of the resin once it is cured. There are so many different polyester resins, each containing additives for specific application that it is important to know what you are using.

Epoxy Resins

The epoxy resins have developed in recent years at a fantastic rate and exhibit such superior storage, strength and handling properties that their relatively higher cost appears to be the main factor limiting their complete replacement of the polyesters in the sculptor's studio.

The molecular structure of the thermosetting epoxies is such that they are relatively unaffected by exposure to air and atmospheric conditions before curing. Because of this condition they have an unlimited shelf life and react more consistently during hardening and cur-

DIAGRAM 14.

1. Polyester resin with inhibitor and cobalt.
2. Added "catalyst" breaks down the inhibitor.
3. Cobalt decomposes the catalyst releasing free radicals.
4. Free radicals spark the cross-linking of the polyester molecules without the aid of pressure or heat.

INHIBITOR CATALYST

MOLECULAR CHAIN COBALT

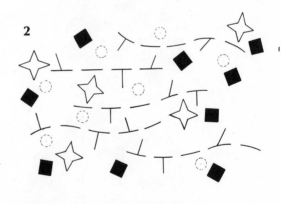

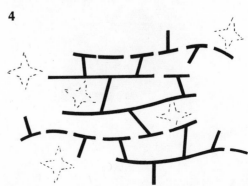

ing than the polyesters. The cured epoxies exhibit very complex cross-linked systems induced by a variety of curing agents including amines, acids and other resins. Since there are so many cross-linking possibilities, a great variety of epoxy resins is being produced.

At present one of the most effective uses for epoxies is as super adhesives. Epoxies in thin liquids, viscous liquids and filled putties combined with liquid and pastelike hardeners, are unsurpassed for bonding a variety of similar and dissimilar materials. The heat-cured epoxy adhesives usually have higher mechanical strength than those cured

at room temperature but regardless of the curing methods they are infusible and insoluble, and are unaffected by aging and weather.

Quick setting epoxy coatings applied by either brushing or spraying, impart to almost any material a long-lasting, tough, hard, flexible surface that is waterproof and resistant to strong chemicals as well as extremes of weather. Cast epoxies show less shrinkage on curing than the polyesters. Fibrous-glass reinforced epoxy laminates exhibit greatly increased tensile strength, bending strength and stiffness as compared to the polyester laminates.

1. Fiberglass cloth is draped over a temporary support of wire and crumpled paper towels.

2. The cloth is saturated with resin and reinforced with laminations of mat and more cloth.

3. Part of the original form is cut away and some new forms are added.

4. After a metal support is laminated into the base, surface texture and color are added.

5. The completed sculpture.

(Photographs by the author)

STUDENT EXERCISES WITH FIBERGLASS

Because of the many steps involved and the medium's inherent lack of character, students are usually hesitant about starting their first fiberglass sculpture. Wood has a grain they can follow and the wood stands there waiting to be carved. Clay begs to be modeled and it quickly takes shape in the hand. Fiberglass and polyester resin, however, give no hint of their formal potential, leaving the novice in a quandary as to what should be done with this *stuff*. The photographs on the next page show a student's first venture with the medium.

Fiberglass Sculpture by student, Ohio University

1

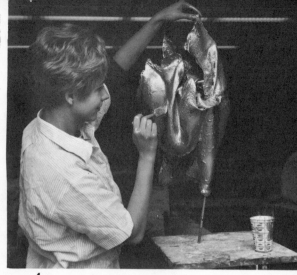

4

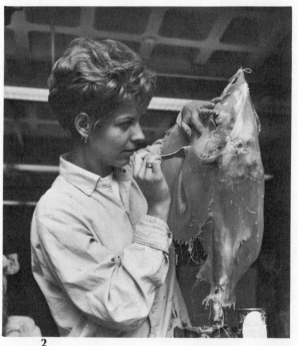

2

3

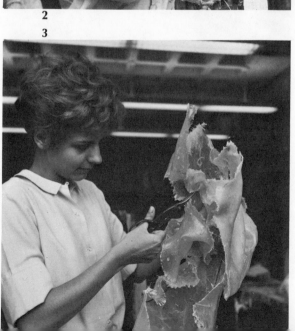

5

95

SENTRY by John Baldwin
FIBERGLASS
(Photograph by Doug Stewart)

SAMOTHRACIAN (three views) by John Baldwin

FIBERGLASS

(Photograph by Doug Stewart)

REINFORCEMENTS, FILLERS AND ADDITIVES

The synthetic resins are seldom used for sculpture without a reinforcement, filler or an additive of some kind. Except where the transparence or translucence of the pure resin is an important factor as in the solid acrylics, fillers and reinforcements contribute in so many ways to the working characteristics and to the structural properties of the resins that the loss of optical clarity seems a minor disadvantage. Additives alter and adapt the resins for special conditions.

If we take concrete as an analogy, the cement, like the resin, serves as a binder while the sand and gravel are fillers that add strength and body to the mix and at the same time lower the cost. To increase the tensile and flexural strength of concrete a grid of steel rods is imbedded. This grid is a reinforcement. If the job is such that more than the normal time is required to pour and work the concrete, a retarder is added that delays the setting time. The retarding agent is an additive.

Reinforcements

The reinforcement material best suited for use with the low-pressure, air-cured resins is fibrous glass. It accounts for 90 percent of all the reinforcements used. Other reinforcing materials are cheaper than glass and have special advantages for specific jobs in industry, but their relatively poor handling and physical properties limit their usefulness for the sculptor.

Asbestos fiber functions mostly as a filler. It is also available as a woven fabric, mat and roving. It is useful where resistance to high heat is essential, but it does not handle well and therefore is suitable only for relatively simple forms. Cotton fabrics are useful only in high-pressure laminates but of little value for hand lay-up methods of the sculptor. Sisal is a low-cost, cellulosic fiber useful in some molding operations but does not have the excellent handling and physical properties of fibrous glass. It also absorbs moisture.

The tensile strength of a reinforcement depends directly upon the strength of the individual filament, its continuity, weave and pattern. The tensile strength of minute glass fibers with diameters of only 0.00020 to 0.00100 inch is about 400,000 pounds per square inch. However, due to the damage caused in the handling and processing, relative to spinning and weaving, a more realistic rating of 250,000 p.s.i. is given for fibrous glass as a useful reinforcing material. These fine fibers are obtained by forcing molten glass through extremely small jets. Then this extruded material is wafted by a current of air or steam, forming short, attenuated staple fibers. To make an extremely thin continuous filament, the fiber is pulled mechanically at very high speeds from the orifice.

Up to 240 of these filaments are gathered together into bundles to make "strands" for woven fabrics. During the production of the filaments they are treated with a size that protects them from abrasion, helps bond the filaments together and primes them for saturation by the resin. Since one pound of woven strands consists of approximately 800 square feet of surface, this expanse of surface must be prepared to receive the resin, just as it is necessary to clean a surface before painting. The size or the abrasion protection is burned off after the fabric has been woven and then a primer or coupling agent is applied that facilitates resin saturation. This primer is known as a "finish." Since there is less handling in producing mats, rovings

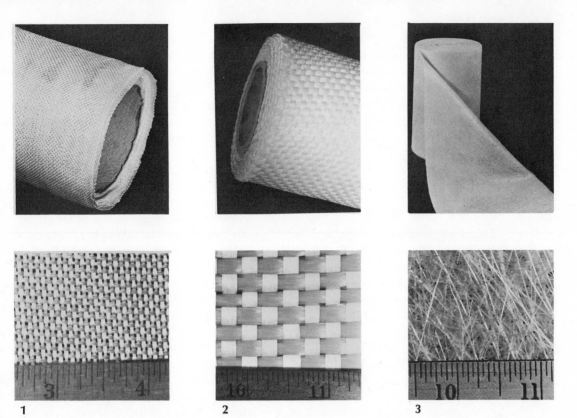

1. Woven fabrics and tapes provide the highest strength and are the most costly of the fibrous glass reinforcements. They come in a wide variety of weight, thickness, compactness and coarseness of "strand," and the weave varies in the number of "strands" per inch and the dominance of direction. In unidirectional types there are more "strands" running in one direction than the other, providing greater strength in that direction.

2. Woven roving is a thick, coarse fabric made of the rope-like roving. It is cheaper than the finer fabrics.

3. Reinforcing mat consists of swirled, continuous strands or chopped strands layered in a random pattern. There are overlay mats that are fragile and soft but conform easily to any complex form, and there are surfacing mats that are stiffer, hold together better and are prepared to give a finer surface.

4. Chopped strands, ¼ inch - ½ inch in length are available in bags, and make a cheap reinforcing filler.

(Photographs courtesy of Owens-Corning Fiberglas)

and chopped strands, they do not require the protective size treatment. Therefore a single bonding size and coupling agent can be used, making for greater economy in production costs. It is important that the coupling agent be designed specifically for the resin to be reinforced. Some reinforcements are treated especially for either polyester, epoxy or the phenolic resins.

Fillers and Additives

Fillers are used with resins to extend the material and lower the cost of production. However, fillers play a more significant role than mere economy in the production of reinforced plastic articles, including sculpture. Fillers become an integral part of the finished plastic form and impart additional strength, toughness, fire and heat resistance, and color. They also contribute in a positive way to the molding, forming, and machining characteristics of a plastic. Fillers are seldom used in resins when laminating fibrous glass or other reinforcements as they impede the saturation of the glass material, and the reinforcement itself provides ample filler. An absorbent filler like diatomaceous earth will thicken the resin more quickly than a less absorbing filler such as asbestos shorts or fine wood chips. Thus the amount and kind of filler will determine the brushing or troweling characteristics of the filled resin.

In some instances fillers can constitute up to 90 percent of the mixture. The exact proportion of filler to resin depends on the filler, the resin and the desired properties in the finished form. Over-saturation of the resin will decrease the strength proportionately.

The cellulose fillers (paper and wood) show the highest rates of water absorption in a tank-tested, cured resin (up to 4.75 percent), while mineral fillers showed only 0.5 percent water absorption for the same period of submersion. Fillers in sufficient amounts lessen the shrinkage that occurs in resins when they are cast in molds, thus decreasing internal stresses and crazing.

Before using any filler it is wise to experiment with it in small batches to test its working characteristics and also to determine the percentage that gives the optimum results. Most fillers retard the setting of the catalyzed resin in thin applications. Carbon black is an especially potent retarder. China clay is another. On the other hand, calcium carbonate accelerates the setting time. In thicker applications of the resin, most fillers tend to accelerate catalyzation.

Thixotropicity, the resistance to gravitational pull of a liquid on a vertical surface, is improved by the use of some fillers such as china clay and fine silica. *Thixo Gel, Cab-O-Sil* and *Sylodex* are three commercial fillers that make resins more thixotropic. The flammability of a plastic can be cut down with the use of fire-resistant fillers such as asbestos fibers and metallic powders as well as commercial additives that make the plastic self-extinguishing.

The increased opacity of the resin caused by most fillers minimizes the harmful effects of ultraviolet rays on work to be exhibited out-of-doors. There are colorless commercial additives available that filter the ultraviolet light without imparting color or reducing the clarity of the resin. *Uvinal* is one such product. Pigments and powdered metals are fillers that improve the color and the overall appearance of plastic sculpture. They also filter out harmful light rays and in the case of the metals, retard flammability.

In general, additives alter the resin so as to improve its specific storage, working, finishing and cured-state characteristics. Stabilizers minimize the degradation or chemical breakdown of a polymer that may occur at any stage from its "cooking" in the laboratory to the final cross-linked thermoset. Antioxidents also prevent degradation in some plastics resulting from contact with atmospheric oxygen. Plasticizers have an effect on polymers similar to heat. By "lubricating" the molecules, they are able to slip and slide over each other, which results in a more flexible plastic. Cobalt accelerates the setting of a catalyzed resin. It is an especially useful additive when working in temperatures below normal. A wax suspended in polyester resins helps bring about a more complete cure by working itself in the surface during the polymeriza-

tion process, forming a seal against atmospheric moisture and oxygen. *Sanding Aid* is a commercial additive that achieves this end. Sanding is simplified because of the elimination of any uncured, gummy surface.

The following lists of fillers is by no means complete but covers those materials available and useful to the sculptor in hand-forming and finishing reinforced plastic sculpture:

List of Fillers

Silica (Synthetic)—Adds thixotropicity to polyester and epoxy resins without opaquing them excessively.

Chopped glass strands—Gives multidirectional strength and body to molding compounds and modeling putties. It is used with melamines, polyesters, epoxies, phenolics and silicones.

Diatomaceous earth (Celite)—Fossilized diatoms used with the above resins for thixotropicity and body where additional strength and light weight is desirable.

Asbestos shorts—Provides mechanical strength, heat and flame resistance and a buttery consistency for polyester modeling putties.

Calcium carbonate (chalk)—In crystalline form it increases tensile strength and mar resistance, mixes excellently and produces a high-sheen finish.

Calcium silicate—Adds thixotropicity to polyesters. Provides a smooth, transparent surface and low water absorption.

Clay (Kaolinite)—Provides reduced shrinkage, improved machinability, smoothness and excellent physical properties in polyester and epoxy molding compounds.

Pigments—Usually used in combination with other fillers or extenders to impart color to polyester, epoxy and other resins. They also serve to filter harmful light rays.

Powdered metals—Add body and opacity as well as a metalic lustre to polyester, epoxy and other resins.

Sawdust—Useful as an extender in polyester and epoxy molding and modeling formulations where a texture is desirable. It machines and finishes easily.

Wood flour—Controls shrinkage in molding compounds and adds impact resistance. It disperses evenly throughout the resin, finishes well and is cheap.

1

2

3

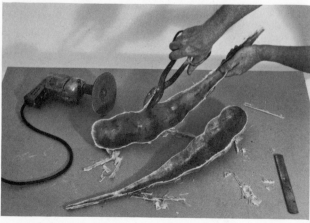

4

MOLDING AND CASTING

Glass-reinforced polyester resin is easily molded or cast. Industry has developed many techniques for mass-producing useful items in this strong, light material. A variety of open and closed molds capable of molding pressures ranging from zero to 3000 pounds per square inch and temperatures ranging from 70° to 350°F produce such objects as tiny electrical components, large boat hulls, storage tanks, automobile bodies and rocket housings.

As is usually the case, the simplest methods relying on the smallest amount of costly equipment but utilizing the greatest amount of hand labor (costly for industry), are those most practical for the molding and casting of sculpture. The hand lay-up or spray-up techniques using open molds with no pressure and only room temperature are most practical in the studio. Not having to withstand high pressures, the molds can be cheaply made out of

1. Both halves of the plaster mold are coated with a commercial mold-release agent. Wax may also be used.

2. Pieces of fiberglass cloth and mat, cut to fit, are placed in the open mold and saturated with catalyzed polyester resin. Because of the complex, curved surfaces, a brush is used. All of the air bubbles must be brushed out. On large simple surfaces a roller or squeegee is practical for spreading the resin and working out the air pockets.

3. When the resin has set, each laminated section is removed from the mold.

4. The edges are trimmed with metal shears, rasps and sandpaper. The best time to trim a fiberglass laminate is immediately after the resin has gelled. In the gelatinous state, a mat knife cuts it with ease.

plaster, wood, sheet metal, and even cardboard.

The same methods employed for casting plaster or cement may be used for casting polyester resin. Open molds, piece molds, waste molds, and silicone-rubber flex molds are filled with the catalyzed resin and allowed to stand until the resin has set. The resin is used with or without fillers and reinforcements depending upon the size of the sculpture, the strength needed and the degree of translucence desired.

Pure polyester resin cast or molded in thick sections will generate a lot of exotherm as the resin polymerizes. Too much heat can cause cracking and warping. Fillers added to the resin will control this condition by cutting down the amount of heat generated. Fillers also reduce the amount of shrinkage in a cast or molded form. Remember, less catalyst is needed to polymerize polyester resin in thick castings or laminations than in thin ones. Too much catalyst increases the exotherm.

The series of photographs on these pages shows the hand lay-up, open-molding technique using a two-piece plaster mold.

(Photographs by the author)

Untitled Sculpture by Pat Kelly

MOLDED FIBERGLASS

(Photograph by Doug Stewart)

5

5. Both molded halves are cemented together with a putty made of polyester resin, calcium silicate and chopped glass-strands. Surface imperfections are filled with this same putty. When completely cured, this form was sanded and sprayed with several coats of high-gloss automobile paint. A sculpture created in this manner is shown on this page.

STATISTIC (detail) by John Baldwin

FIBERGLASS, BURLAP, POLYESTER RESIN

(Photograph by Doug Stewart)

ECHELON by John Baldwin

FIBERGLASS, POLYESTER RESIN AND ALUMI-
NUM POWDER OVER CARDBOARD

(Photograph by Doug Stewart)

SURFACING AND COLORING

The natural color and texture of fiberglass-reinforced plastic is about as interesting as a varnished soda cracker. Therefore, it is seldom used without the addition of coloring agents and fillers that give life and character to otherwise insipid and lackluster surfaces. Coloring agents are mixed directly into the resin before the catalyst or hardener is added and they become an integral part of the reinforced plastic. They are not surface colors but go as deep as that part of the lamination to which the colored resin has been applied.

Colorants

In open molding, the coloring agent is usually added to a gel-coat that is painted or sprayed into the mold first. This gel-coat is allowed to set up before any glass reinforcement is added. When the piece is removed from the mold, the colored gel-coat is on the surface of the form. This is the technique followed for coloring open-molded boats. However, hand-built fiberglass sculpture is usually colored after all the forming is completed since these are built from the inside armature, or support, outward toward the "skin."

Commercial coloring agents are pigments and dyes suspended or dispersed in a polymer base, ready to use, and available in jars and tubes. These colorants are very potent. A small amount will color quite a bit of resin. Each color should be tested to learn its particular potency. Dry, powdered pigments may also be used to color polyester resin. These must be ground into the resin before the hardener is added.

There are three types of colorants used with the synthetic resins: dyes, organic pigments and inorganic pigments. In general, the dyes are the least stable when exposed to light and heat. However, they are more transparent than the pigments because dyes absorb and *transmit* rays of light while pigments absorb and *reflect* them. The inorganic pigments are considered the most permanent. But each pigment must be taken separately as each will react differently in regard to exposure to light, heat and the vehicle in which it is suspended. In recent years some organic pigments have been developed that are superior to the inorganic pigments.

The following pigments have been proven stable in polyester and fiberglass laminates and are widely used in the plastics industry.

COLORS	SOURCE
Black, yellow, red	(Iron oxide)
Ceramic black	
Chrome green	
Ultramarine blue	
Turquoise	(Chrome, cobalt, alumina)
Yellow, buff	(Nickel, titanium)
Ceramic yellows	(Antimony, titanium, chrome oxide)
Molybdate orange	
Chrome orange, yellow	
Manganese violet	
Pink	(Chrome, tin)
Maroon, red, orange	(Cadmium mercury)
Maroon, red, orange	(Cadmium sulfo-selenide)
Titanium white	
Blue, green	(Phthalocyanine)

Metallic powders mixed with thermo-setting resins impart a bright metallic luster to the finished laminates that can hardly be distinguished from cast metals. These metallic-filled surfaces can be antiqued and patinated by rubbing them with darker colors. "Chrysalis" by Lily Landis on page 21 is an aluminum-filled, epoxy resin and fiberglass sculpture. The color plates "Alchemy" page 72 and "Trophy" page 85 are good examples of a patinated, bronze-filled, polyester resin finish.

Prepared enamels and lacquers may be applied to the hard, cured surface of reinforced plastic laminates. With successive coatings, sandings and buffing, a high-gloss, auto-body finish is possible, as shown by Pat Kelly's molded sculptures on pages 85 and 103. If a semi-mat, mottled coloring is desired, successive applications of colored resin are applied with a brush or daubed with a rag over a base color. Several of the color plates show this technique. Many of the techniques and tricks of the painter are useful in coloring and finishing fiberglass sculpture. The color plate on page 104 — "Masquerade" — shows many of these techniques utilized in one sculpture.

Textures

Textures are achieved by mixing any grease-free, dry filler to the catalyzed resin. The quality of the texture will depend on the coarseness of the filler.

Texturing materials may also be applied dry to the freshly coated surface before the resin sets. Sawdust, dry ground coffee and sand are typical of the kinds of material that may be used. After the resin has set and the particles are secured to the surface, clear or colored resins should be applied over the texture to seal and protect it.

Cloth and cloth fibers make excellent textures when applied over cured fiberglass surfaces. The fabric itself, such as burlap, can be saturated with catalyzed resin and then reinforced from behind with laminations of fiberglass. "Sentry," page 96 is a good example of this technique. The reinforcement is necessary because cotton, burlap, linen and other fabrics become very brittle when the resin sets. The resin alone imparts about as much strength to these materials as varnish or glue would. The glass fibers provide the real strength. You may run tests to prove this to yourself by coating various fabrics with catalyzed resin. When the resin has cured, compare their flexural and impact strength to a piece of fiberglass cloth that has been saturated and cured.

Thick putties can be made by adding fillers directly to the catalyzed resin. These thick mixtures can be troweled and modeled like plaster or clay. Not only are these putties capable of imparting rich textures to the surfaces of fiberglass sculpture but new forms can be built up also. These putties can also be modeled on an armature.

1. A coloring agent is stirred into the resin. When it is thoroughly dispersed, the drops of hardener will be added and it will be stirred again. The catalyzed, colored resin may be used in a fiberglass laminate or painted over an already cured form as a surface coating.

(Photograph by the author)

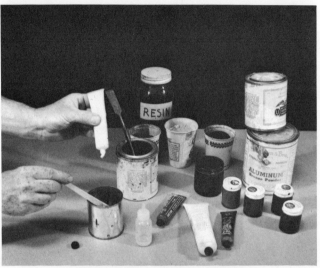

2. Fiberglass chopped strands are added slowly to an already catalyzed resin. The combination of fillers used will depend on the body, thixotropicity, texture and degree of transparence desired.

(Photograph by the author)

3. A variety of textures in one piece of fiberglass reinforced plastic sculpture. This detail shows burlap, corrugated cardboard, random glass-mat fibers (melamine-coated), tack heads, putties made with polyester resin and a variety of fillers.

(Photograph by Doug Stewart)

Texture Chart

1. Short lengths of dry nylon yarn are thrown into a thick coat of resin. Subsequent coats of resin saturate the yarn and make it an integral part of the surface.
2. Cardboard chips are imbedded into heavy, wet resin.
3. Dry nylon yarn is pressed into a sawdust and calcium silicate-filled resin.
4. Burlap saturated with resin. Burlap and other fabrics must be backed with fiberglass for strength.
5. Fiberglass cloth.
6. Fiberglass mat (melamine-coated) produces an interesting random pattern.
7. Resin filled with asbestos fibers applied with a spatula.
8. Sawdust sprinkled dry on a surface freshly coated with resin. When the resin sets a second coat is applied over the sawdust.
9. Chopped fiberglass strands and calcium silicate make a heavy putty capable of being modeled.

WOMAN CLEAR by Thelma Newman

CAST POLYESTER RESIN

BLIND GIRL by James Kearns

CAST FIBERGLASS

(Photograph by Oliver Baker)

WATER SPRITE by Ted Egri

FIBERGLASS AND POLYESTER
RESIN OVER URATHANE FOAM

(Photograph by Laval)

1. Temporary supports for the angel's wings are made of wood, cardboard and hardware cloth. In the background is the ¼-scale model of the fountain and its full-scale armature in hardware cloth.

A SCULPTURE COMMISSION

A sculpture commission entails the acceptance of a set of restrictions over and above those normally imposed by the medium and those the artist arbitrarily imposes upon himself. Commissioned sculpture should be scaled to the particular site or building where it is to be located and it should also relate to it aesthetically. This does not mean that the sculpture should be sub-servient or "blend" into its surroundings. Harmony is not the only aesthetic consideration. What about conflict? The important thing is that the sculpture and the architecture, or site, complement each other so that they are better together than either would be alone. Some of our greatest sculpture has been complementing buildings and *piazze* since earliest times.

There are also thematic limitations imposed if the sculpture is to express something relative to a particular religious belief, a social order, or reflect the function of the building where it is located—a Hall of Justice, a fortress, or a church. It may also commemorate an individual or group.

The sculpture commission illustrated in this series of photographs imposed some specific restrictions and limitations that had to be considered from the very first sketches. It was to be a commemorative monument for an individual and it was to be located in the lobby, or general waiting area, of a busy hospital. The theme had to relate to that passage in the Bible which describes the healing waters in the pool at Bethesda (the name of the hospital). "For an angel went down . . . and troubled the water." *John*—V: 2-4. It was also specified that there be running water and a particular patinated bronze finish. Time was also a limiting factor since it had to be already installed when the hospital was scheduled for completion—eight months hence.

After the preliminary drawings, renderings and an accurate ¼ scale model were completed and approved, work was begun on the full scale sculpture. Most of the techniques described in the previous sections on fiberglass sculpture were used at some stage in this work. The photographs on these pages show the development of this sculptured fountain from the building of the first temporary supports to the finished work installed, its "troubled waters" flowing.

2

4

3

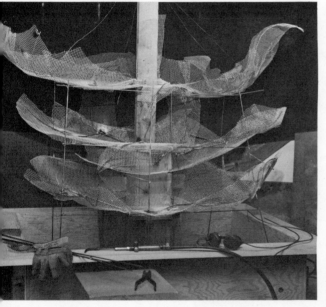

5

2. An assistant laminates fiberglass cloth and mat over the armature of the wings.

3. The angel at an early stage. The head was modeled in clay and cast in fiberglass.

4. The fountain forms in hardware cloth, representing the "troubled waters," are reinforced with a temporary structure of welded steel rods before any fiberglass is applied.

5. Fiberglass cloth and fiberglass mat were laminated over the hardware cloth. When the resin was set the hardware cloth and steel supports were removed.

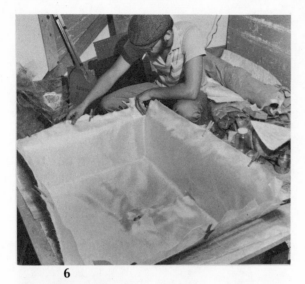

6

7

8

6. An assistant arranges fiberglass cloth and fiberglass mat in a waxed wood form the exact size and shape of the pool.

7. The fiberglass cloth and mat are saturated with catalyzed polyester resin. When set, the fiberglass form was removed from the wood mold, then textured and colored.

8. Patinating the bronze-finished angel.

(Photographs by the author)

Gorsuch Memorial Fountain, Bethesda Hospital,
Zanesville, Ohio, by John Baldwin

FIBERGLASS

(Photograph by Doug Stewart)

HEALTH AND SAFETY
IN HANDLING PLASTICS

Most of the materials and equipment in the artist's studio require a common-sense approach so far as health and safety are concerned. Some pigments are poisonous, some solvents are skin irritants, and most solvents are flammable. Cutting and carving tools are dangerous if not properly handled and all power tools must be used with caution.

The new plastics, like everything else in the studio, should be handled carefully. The warnings and cautions that appear on the containers should be heeded as they are placed there for *your* health and safety.

A few people are sensitive to some of the ingredients used in formulating synthetic resins. They should avoid all contact with them. However, most people are not allergic to the resins and if minimum care is taken they will experience no harmful effects. Most of the common solvents used by artists—turpentine, thinner, petroleum solvents, alcohol, etc. — are capable of causing dermatitis, and some are toxic. If protective gloves cannot be worn due to the nature of the work (few artists can work wearing gloves), frequent washing with soap and water followed by a restorative hand cream is the best protection against skin irritation. Avoid spilling or splashing the resins, solvents and catalyst — especially on yourself. If this does happen, immediately wash off the area with soap and water. It is wise to keep most of the body covered while working.

There are many variables in determining the potential toxicity or fire hazard of a particular material: the amount of material to be handled, the frequency of contact, the amount of ventilation and temperature in the work area, the concentration of fumes and the flammability of the material are some that should be considered.

The greatest hazard of toxicity occurs during the manufacture of the basic ingredients. The quantity is usually great and the concentration of fumes is potentially high. On the other hand, the sculptor is usually involved with relatively small amounts of synthetic material capable of emitting only weak concentrations of fumes. The dust from machining plastics can cause skin, throat and lung irritation and the tiny fiberglass particles that float in the air can cause a rash on sensitive skin. Close-weave protective clothing, frequent washing and good ventilation are recommended. Always use a dust mask when sanding cured fiberglass laminates.

Care should be taken in storing resins, solvents, catalysts and modifying agents. Keep them separate in a cool place where they cannot spill. Always use clean mixing cans and cups. Never mix a promoter (cobalt) directly into a catalyst. An explosion might result. Always mix the promoter into the resin before the catalyst is added. Keep catalysts away from flame and heat. Water, sand and a good carbon dioxide or dry chemical extinguisher should be within easy reach.

This might seem like such a frightening list of *do's, don'ts* and *warnings* that you would prefer to try your hand at some other medium. Don't be hasty. Just remember that similar hazards exist in photography, etching, lithography, ceramics, and painting.

CITADEL by John Baldwin

FIBERGLASS

(Photograph by Doug Stewart)

BIBLIOGRAPHY

Althouse, A. D. and C. H. Turnquist. *Modern Welding Practice.* The Goodheart-Willcox Co., Chicago, 1958.

Bowness, Alan. *Modern Sculpture.* E. P. Dutton and Company, Inc., New York, 1965.

Contemporary Sculpture. (Arts Yearbook 8) Art Digest, Inc., New York, 1965.

Fiberglas Reinforced Plastics. Bulletin of the Owens-Corning Fiberglas Corporation, November 1964.

Hunter, Sam. *Modern Painting and Sculpture.* Dell Publishing Co., Inc., New York, 1959.

Kinney, Gilbert Ford. *Engineering Properties and Applications of Plastics.* John Wiley & Sons, Inc., New York, 1957.

Modern Plastics Encyclopedia 1963. Plastics Catalogue Corporation, New York, 1962.

Newman, Thelma R. *Plastics as an Art Form.* Chilton Company, Philadelphia, 1964.

Read, Herbert. *A Concise History of Modern Sculpture.* Frederick A. Praeger, Inc., New York, 1964.

Rich, Jack C. *The Materials and Methods of Sculpture.* Oxford University Press, Inc., New York, 1947.

Ritchie, Andrew C. *Sculpture of the Twentieth Century.* The New York Museum of Modern Art, New York, 1952.

Struppeck, Jules. *The Creation of Sculpture.* Holt-Rinehart and Winston, Inc., New York, 1952.

Wakeman, Reginald L. *The Chemistry of Commercial Plastics.* Reinhold Publishing Corp., New York, 1947.

Welding and Cutting Manual. Linde Air Products Company, New York, 1949.

SUPPLIERS AND MANUFACTURERS

The materials and supplies needed to make sculpture of welded metal or fiberglass reinforced plastics are not to be found in the local art shops among the traditional artist materials. Being industrial materials, they are obtained instead from suppliers and jobbers listed in the yellow pages of your local telephone directory. The list below is by no means complete and is offered only as a start in your search for a source of supply.

Many large cities have at least one supply house like the O.K.I. Supply Company of Cincinnati, Ohio, where everything necessary for the industrial welder is available. In Detroit the Cadillac Plastic and Chemical Company has everything one needs for laminating and molding reinforced plastics. Some of the large merchandising chains and mail-order houses offer a limited selection of welding equipment and fiberglass supplies. Most large manufacturers are not set up to fill small orders. For them anything less than a carload is difficult to audit. However, all of the manufacturers listed below will help you to locate distributors of their products in your area.

OXY-ACETYLENE WELDING

Equipment and Supplies

Air Reduction Sales Company
Airco Welding Products Division
P.O. Box 2
Union, New Jersey

Dockson Corporation
3851 Wabash Avenue
Detroit 8, Michigan

Linde Air Products Company
30 East 42nd Street
New York 17, New York

Marquette Corporation
5075 Wayzata Boulevard
Minneapolis, Minnesota

O.K.I. Supply Company
7730 Reinhold Drive
Cincinnati, Ohio

Smith Welding Equipment Company
Division of Tescom Corporation
2633 S.E. 4th Street
Minneapolis 14, Minnesota

Victor Equipment Company
Flame Welding and Cutting Apparatus Division
Denton, Texas

ARC WELDING

Equipment and Supplies

Hobart Brothers Company, Inc.
Box 10
Troy, Ohio

Jackson Products
5523 Nine Mill Road
Warren, Michigan

Lincoln Electric Company
22777 St. Clair Avenue
Cleveland, Ohio

Westinghouse Electric Corporation
Welding Department
Box 225-T
Buffalo, New York

METAL FLAME SPRAY

Equipment and Supplies

Metalizing Company of America, Inc.
Department T.R.
3520 West Carrol Avenue
Chicago 24, Illinois

Metco, Incorporated
1101 Prospect Avenue
Westbury, Long Island, New York

FIBERGLASS REINFORCED PLASTICS

Reinforcing Materials (Fibrous Glass)

Ferro Corporation
Fiber Glass Division
Nashville 11, Tennessee

Fiber Glass Industries Incorporated
Amsterdam, New York

Modiglass Fibers, Incorporated
Bremen, Ohio

Owens-Corning Fiberglas Corporation
Toledo 1, Ohio

Polyester Resins

American Cyanamid Company
Plastics and Resins Division
Wallingford, Connecticut

Glidden Company
Coating and Resins Group
900 Union Commerce Building
Cleveland 14, Ohio

Interchemical Corporation
Finishes Division
1255 Broad Street
Clifton, New Jersey

Reichold Chemicals, Incorporated
525 North Broadway
White Plains, New York

Rohm & Haas Company
222 West Washington Square
Philadelphia 5, Pennsylvania

United States Rubber Company
Naugatuck Chemical Division
Naugatuck, Connecticut

Epoxy Resins

Reichold Chemicals, Incorporated
525 North Broadway
White Plains, New York

Ren Plastics, Incorporated
5656 South Cedar Street
Lansing, Michigan

Shell Chemical Company
Plastics and Resins Division
110 West 51st Street
New York 20, New York

Steelcote Manufacturing Company
3118 Gratiot Street
St. Louis 3, Missouri

Union Carbide Plastics Company
Division of Union Carbide Corporation
270 Park Avenue
New York 17, New York

Catalysts (Hardeners) and Promotors

Lucidol Division
Wallace & Tiernan, Incorporated
1740 Military Road
Buffalo 5, New York

McKesson & Robbins
Chemical Department
155 East 44th Street
New York 17, New York

Shell Chemical Company
Plastics and Resins Division
110 West 51st Street
New York 20, New York

U. S. Peroxygen Corporation
850 Morton Street
Richmond, California

Modifiers and Additives
Pigments, Coloring Agents, Gel-coats

Ferro Corporation
Color Division
4150 East 56th Street
Cleveland 5, Ohio

The Glidden Company
Pigments and Color Division
3901 Hawkins Point Road
Baltimore 26, Maryland

Plastic Molders Supply Company
74 South Avenue
Fanwood, New Jersey

Whittaker, Clark & Daniels, Incorporated
100 Church Street
New York, New York

Plasticizers
Flexol DOP

Union Carbide & Carbon Company
Plastics Company Division
270 Park Avenue
New York 17, New York

Plastolein

Emery Industries, Incorporated
Carew Tower
Cincinnati, Ohio

Ultra-violet Absorbers

Antara Chemicals
General Aniline & Film Corporation
435 Hudson Street
New York 14, New York

Geigy Industrial Chemicals Oivision
Geigy Chemical Corporation
Ardsley, New York

Fillers

Chemtron Fiberglass Company
El Monte, California

Johns-Manville
22 East 40th Street
New York 16, New York

Miller-Stephenson Chemical Company
Danbury, Connecticut

Thixotropic Agents
Cabo-O-Sil

Cabot Corporation
Minerals and Chemicals Division
125 High Street
Boston 10, Massachusetts

Thixogel

Interchemical Corporation
Finishes Division
1255 Broad Street
Clifton, New Jersey

Fire Retardants

Hooker Chemicals Company
39 Iroquois Street
Niagara Falls, New York

McKesson & Robbins
Chemicals Department
155 East 44th Street
New York 17, New York

Mold Release Agents
Fluoro Glide

Chemplast, Incorporated
3 Central Avenue
East Newark, New Jersey

Partall

Rexco Chemicals Company
11602 Anabel Avenue
Garden Grove, California

Sil-A-Spray and No-Stick
Ellen Products Company, Incorporated
131 South Liberty Drive
Stony Point, New York

Adhesives
Devcon Corporation
Danvers, Massachusetts

Ren Plastics Incorporated
5656 South Cedar Street
Lansing, Michigan

Solvents
Acetone
Shell Chemical Company
110 West 51st Street
New York, New York

Ren Cleaner
Ren Plastics, Incorporated
5656 South Cedar Street
Lansing, Michigan

Styrene Monomer
Allied Chemical Corporation
Plastics Division
40 Rector Street
New York 6, New York

Fiberglass-Evercoat Company, Incorporated
Cornell Road
Cincinnati, Ohio

Union Carbide Chemicals Company
Division of Union Carbide Corporation
270 Park Avenue
New York 17, New York

INDEX